The HEALING POWER OF PRAYER *for the* MIND, BODY & SOUL

All scripture quotations are from the King James Version of the Bible.

The Healing Power of Prayer for the Mind, Soul and Body by Joy Haney
© 1996
Radiant Life Publications, Stockton, California

First printing, September 1996

All rights reserved. No portion of this publication may be reproduced, stored in an electronic system, or transmitted, in any form or by any means, electronic, mechanical, photocopying, recording, or otherwise without the prior written permission of the publisher except in the case of brief quotations in articles and reviews.

ISBN: 0-1-880969-24-6

Printed in the United States of America.

Dedication

I lovingly dedicate this book to my husband, Kenneth Haney, and our five children, their spouses and the grandchildren.

TABLE OF CONTENTS

Foreword		7
Preface		9
1.	The Recent Phenomenon of Prayer	15
2.	What Doctors Say About Prayer	27
3.	What the Greats Say About God and Prayer	45
4.	What is Prayer and How Important is It?	57
5.	The Healing Power of Prayer for the Mind	79
6.	The Healing Power of Prayer for the Body	95
7.	The Healing Power of Prayer for the Soul	113
8.	Guidance for Everyday Life Through Prayer	131
9.	Modern-Day Answers to Prayer	143
Notes		157

Foreword

The Healing Power of Prayer for the Mind, Body and Soul is an excellent book for all who desire a release from the tenacious grip of insecurity, anxiety, fear or pain. With Great wisdom, direction, experience, and grace, Joy Haney illuminates and inspires one to the process of prayer as quite simple—all that is needed is a desire for communication with God.

Prayer necessity and power is documented by numerous examples of historical use throughout the ages, a current resurgence of interest in the healing power of prayer, and personal testimonies which verify when people pray—God answers. This book is a remarkable gem and vital encouragement for living in such stressful times. What a comfort to know that we are not alone and that strength/power to endure, peace, comfort, healing, and perhaps miracles are but a prayer away.

Pamela Byrne Hanley, Ph.D., R.N.
Director of Behavior Medicine
Kaiser Permanente
Stockton, CA

The Healing Power of Prayer for the Mind, Body and Soul is inspiring, thought provoking and incredibly uplifting! Cover to cover it will challenge you to open up your heart and soul to a new frontier and greater horizon. Within the pages of this book lie the fundamental truths upon which the world rests. There is a God and He answers prayer. Joy Haney dispels any doubt. If you are searching at all for healing and wholeness, a better lifestyle and mental attitude, physical well-being and spiritual awakening then you must read this book! It will change your whole outlook on life. It will make you want to pray and enjoy getting results."

Rev. Jason W. Sciscoe
Evangelist
Minister of Prayer

Knowledge alone is not enough; it takes passion to utilize the world of knowledge. Joy Haney has a wealth of knowledge from a life of experience, yet it is her passion which causes readers to be taken into a realm where faith is flowing, the impossible is tangible, miracles are a reality and God becomes real. This in turn transforms lives into burning fires which consume doubts, and light up their worlds with the message that all things are possible to the people who know how to pray.

In this book you will learn to whom you should direct your prayers, and what to expect concerning them. May heaven bless you as you raise your voice in prayer to the God of heaven, whose name is the Lord Jesus Christ.

Rev. Nathaniel Haney
President of School of Prophets Ministry
Minister of Prayer

PREFACE

When people have food and fail to feed others who are starving, they commit a crime. If someone has a cure for a certain disease and keeps it a secret, or if someone who has the power to free those who are enslaved and fails to do so, he would be considered cold, heartless, selfish and unconcerned.

That is why this book was written. I have found a dynamic secret: the power of prayer. Because of it my life has literally been changed. It has lifted me into a realm of victory like nothing else on earth. It is my desire that all people have the same privilege.

The following pages are my gift to everyone who lives in this modern generation of unprecedented violence—one that is filled with extreme fear, hate, confusion, greed and terrorism. May the people who do not know how to pray, who are desolate, discouraged and in despair read this book. Let the people who are hungering for more, who have found life to be empty, read this book and be filled.

As Augustine wrote many years ago, "Narrow is the mansion of my soul; enlarge Thou it, that Thou mayest enter in."

In a world that has grown smaller and the thinking ability of many people has diminished into hate, suspicion and fear, may their souls expand once more with love and power. If there has never been love, may this book kindle a desire to enter into the dimension of true love, which is found in God.

Helen Keller once wrote, "If the blind put their hand in God's, they find their way more surely than those who see but have not faith or purpose."

Putting your hand into God's hand is done through prayer. No special tools are needed for prayers to be made. It requires no degrees, no audiences, no buildings, no permits, no priests, no ministers, no clothes, no money; nothing is needed to address God but a heart of faith and reverence.

As prayer has enriched my life, may your life be enriched as you *daily* offer up prayers and thanksgiving. As fish cannot live without water, neither can human beings truly live without communing with their Creator.

"Learn from the Camel"
The camel at the close of the day,
Kneels down upon the sandy plain
To have his burden lifted off
And rest again.
My soul, thou too shouldst fall to thy knees
When daylight draweth to a close,
And let thy Master lift the load

And give repose.
The camel knees at morning's dawn
To have the guide replace his load
Then rises up anew, to take
The desert road....

"The man without prayer is as the fish out of water, and gasping for life."

S. Chrysotom

CHAPTER 1

THE RECENT PHENOMENON OF PRAYER

The June 24, 1996, issue of *Time Magazine* reported the following:

> A Time/CNN poll of 1,004 Americans conducted last week by Yankelovich Partners found that 82% believed in the healing power of prayer; 73% believed that praying for someone else can help cure their illness; 77% believed that God sometimes intervenes to cure people who have a serious illness, and 64% thought doctors should pray with those patients who request it.

Time also stated that Dr. Herbert Benson, a researcher on prayer, reported in his latest book, *Timeless Healing*, that in a five-year study, it was discovered that patients using meditation (and claimed to feel the intimate presence of a higher power) to battle chronic illnesses had better health and more rapid recoveries. "Our genetic blueprint has made believing in an Infinite Absolute part of our nature," wrote Benson. He said that "humans are wired for God."

Benson's research led him to believe that prayer operates along the same biochemical pathways as the relaxation response. In other words, praying affects epinephrine and other corticosteroid messengers or stress hormones, leading to lower blood pressure, a more relaxed heart rate and respiration and other benefits.

In the same article, David Felten, chairman of the Department of Neurobiology at the University of Rochester, was quoted as saying, "Anything involved with meditation and controlling the state of mind that alters hormone activity has the potential to have an impact on the immune system."

Not only was the subject of prayer explored and discussed in *Time*, but *Newsweek* blazed this across the front cover of the January 6, 1992, issue: "Talking to God–An Intimate Look at the Way We Pray."

Newsweek reported that according to recent studies at NORC, a national research center, by Andrew M. Greeley, the sociologist-novelist-priest, more than three quarters (78%) of all Americans pray at least once a week; more than half (57%) report praying at least once a day.

THE HEALING POWER OF PRAYER

The authors of the article "Talking to God" state the following:

> Some of these prayers are born *in extremis:* there are few atheists in cancer wards or on unemployment lines. But in allegedly rootless, materialistic, self-centered America, there is also a hunger for a personal experience of God that prayer seeks to satisfy. Greeley's studies show that serious prayer usually begins after the age of 30, when the illusion that we are masters of our own fate fades and adults develop a deeper need to call on the Master of the Universe.

David Rosenhan, a professor of law and psychology at Stanford University, was quoted in the *Newsweek* article as saying, "It was very rare two years ago to find vital, vibrant religion on the college campus. Now there are prayer meetings here that are attended by 300 to 500 students regularly."

The front cover of the March 1994 issue of *Life Magazine* featured a picture of a young girl with her hands cupped together in an attitude of prayer, with the caption, "The Power of Prayer," as the cover title. The nine-page article dealing with prayer shared testimonies of what prayer meant to different people with various religious backgrounds.

One of them, John McCain, a U.S. senator who was a fighter pilot in Vietnam and a POW for five-and-a-half years, reported that in a recent *Life* survey, nine out of ten people pray frequently and earnestly, and almost all say

God has answered their prayers. His describes prayer as "...the flight of the alone to the Alone, a conversation between creature and Creator." He further said,

> "Hear my prayer, O Lord, and let my cry come unto thee!" Out of the depths of life the song of the psalmist reaches toward heaven like beseeching hands. In burning words it says what human beings in all lands and ages have tried to say to God. Help me. Heal me. Love me. Inspire me. Save me from my enemies and from myself. And promise me that when my body dies my soul will live forever.

In the modern-day jungle of violence, terrorism and moral decay, people seem to be aware that something is missing. Because of the void, they are groping for something to hang onto—something that will not let them down. Materialism has proven to be empty, people are becoming more and more afraid, and there is a chilling thought or suggestion among the world's population that there is something catastrophic about to take place. Nothing is sure anymore and it is causing people to pray, and if they do not know how to pray, they are seeking to learn.

The *Newsweek* article also included the following startling information:

> Astonishingly, the current edition of *Books in Print* lists nearly 2,000 titles on prayer, meditation and spiritual growth—more than three times the number devoted to sexual intimacy and how to achieve it.

THE HEALING POWER OF PRAYER

"After the Bible," says Werner Mark Linz, president of Crossroad, a major publisher of serious religious books, "books on prayer are our biggest sellers."

The act of prayer has been in practice since the beginning of time. It was, and always has been, an integral part of the structure of men and women's lives.

Poet Issac Watts wrote the following stanza:

> O God, our help in ages past,
> Our hope for years to come,
> Our shelter from the stormy blast,
> And our eternal home.

Prayer to God was needed in ages past and is needed also in years to come. Alexis Carrel, M.D., wrote an article in the March 1941 issue of *Reader's Digest*. He entitled it "Prayer is Power." He penned the following words which were pertinent in 1941, and are still pertinent today.

Today, as never before, prayer is a binding necessity in the lives of men and nations. The lack of emphasis on the religious sense has brought the world to the edge of destruction. Our deepest source of power and perfection has been left miserably undeveloped. Prayer, the basic exercise of the spirit, must be actively practiced in our private lives. The neglected soul of man must be made strong enough to assert itself once more. For if the power of prayer is again released and used in the lives of common men and women; if the spirit declares its aims clearly and boldly, there is yet hope that our prayers for a better world will be answered. [1]

Prayer was still in existence in 1960. In the late '60s there was at Duke's Medical Center a young man named John whom Dr. William Wilson had been treating with traditional psychiatric therapy and techniques. John was a drug-addicted physician. When he was first admitted, he was taking up to 40 tranquilizers a day. After two months of treatment with no discernible progress, there was nothing more the doctor could do.

When John begged him for some more help, Dr. Wilson said, "John, there's nothing else I can do...but maybe there's something God can do."

Why would a doctor say this? Dr. Wilson tells how he went from not believing to believing. "As a man of science in a field where religion was often viewed with skepticism, the idea of a living God had always seemed remote and archaic," he said.

One particular day a friend, who was an internist, came to see him at the Duke University's Medical Center. He said, "You'd think I had everything. Like you, I've just been appointed as a full professor here at the University. I have unlimited access to a huge laboratory, research facilities and library. Journals publish my papers, the government awards me grants. I've got a great wife and nice kids.

"So why," he asked, leaning back with a wry grin, "do I feel so empty inside?" [2]

Dr. Wilson told him he often felt the same way. Then something happened. He [Wilson] went on an eight-day Scouting trip deep in the wilds of northern Minnesota's Quetico Superior Wilderness Area. The trip, a canoe expedition, would take them close to the Canadian border.

While on the trip with his son, the seventh day fell on a Sunday. That morning, according to Scout rules, they all gathered outside for a worship service. That is the day that changed his life. It was a simple message about being clean inside that tapped something deep inside Dr. Wilson.

He wrote, "It suddenly became apparent that the only true way to clean up your life and be completely fulfilled wasn't through science, wasn't through medicine, and wasn't even through psychiatry—it was through God.. And, looking out over those placid waters, I knew that was what I needed and wanted more than anything in the world—for God to come into my life and make me whole.

"Before I knew it, tears were streaming down my face. As the sunset melted into a golden blur, I was overwhelmed, flooded, with God's love. He was truly with me. His Presence filled me with a peace and reassurance I'd never known." [3]

That is why Dr. Wilson gave John the following instructions: "Pray. Just get down on your knees and pray. And don't get up until you've felt God in your life. He's waiting for you. And He wants to help."

Dr. Wilson wrote the following words:

The next morning when I looked in on John, he returned my gaze with eyes as clear and untroubled as the waters of Basswood Lake.

"You can send me home now," he said. "Everything's going to be all right."

So remarkable was John's recovery, I felt it best that he remain in the hospital for a short period of observation. For three days he stayed. Then he went home.

Prayer, to this day, remains my most effective tool in psychiatric treatment and counseling. Now, I pray regularly for every person in my care before and after sessions. I often pray silently during our conversations together. The power of prayer never ceases to amaze me. And its power has not gone unnoticed by others. [4]

In 1995, Harvey Cox, one of the most widely read theologians of our time, who is the Victor Thomas Professor of Religion at Harvard University, wrote in his book *Fire from Heaven* the following words: "A religious renaissance of sorts is under way all over the globe." [5]

He reported that the number of people turning to God and prayer was astounding. "We are definitely in a period of renewed religious vitality, another *great awakening* if you will, with all the promise and peril religious revivals always bring with them, but this time on a world scale." [6]

Prayer has been an integral part of humanity since time began; it will always be. Prayer is the greatest thing a person can do for himself and others, for it is humanity linked with Divinity, asking for assistance and help in the time of need. It is more than asking; it is communicating. It is adoration for Deity. It is power!

William James said it so ably many years ago. He wrote the following words: "We and God must have business one with the other, and in opening our hearts to him our highest destiny is fulfilled."

> "I dressed [treated or operated on] them, and God healed them."
>
> Dr. Ambroise Pare

CHAPTER 2

WHAT DOCTORS SAY ABOUT PRAYER

Desperation in the hearts of people provokes them to reach for help, hope or healing. For thousands of years people have reached for help; human beings are still reaching and searching for help today. Miracles of healing have been in existence since time began and are still happening today. More and more, physicians are becoming increasingly aware of the fact that God and prayer can make a difference in the treatment of their patients. There are many physicians earnestly trying to help their patients achieve optimum health medically, and are working in conjunction with their patients' beliefs in God and prayer.

This is shown in the following *Associated Press* article, which carried a New York dateline:

> Maybe doctors should write, "Go to church weekly" on their prescription pads. Evidence is growing that religion can be good medicine.
>
> "I believe that physicians can and should encourage patients' autonomous religious activities," said Dr. Dale A. Matthews of Georgetown University. "I'm not saying that physicians should supplant clergy or that prayer should supplant Prozac."
>
> Matthews and other researchers presented the latest evidence of the influence of religious belief on health, Sunday at the annual meeting of the American Association for the Advancement of Science.
>
> At least one piece of research raises the possibility that divine intervention is the answer. The controversial study, conducted in San Francisco, randomly divided 393 seriously ill heart patients into two groups. Half were prayed for, half were not, and none knew which group they were in. The prayer recipients suffered fewer health complications.
>
> "This is outside the realm of science," said Dr. Jeffrey S. Levin of Eastern Virginia Medical School. "If God heals, it's a matter of faith. We can't prove it."

Dr. Will Mayo of the world famous Mayo Clinic said the following:

I have seen patients that were dead by all standards. We knew they could not live. But I have seen a minister come to the bedside and do something for him that I could not do, although I have done everything in my professional power. But something touched some immortal spark in him and in defiance of medical knowledge and materialistic common sense, that patient LIVED! [1]

George Schilling, M.D., who practices internal medicine in Stockton, California, made the following statement in an interview I had with him on March 4, 1996:

We have witnessed people who have been made better by prayer and strong belief. Prayer groups have prayed for some of my patients, and the prayer has helped them to be healed or their health improved. I have a couple who have been on the edge of death several times, and it was the prayers of people in prayer groups that have brought them back. I have another terminally ill lady who I am treating, who has cancer of the pancreas. She has strong belief in God and has a group praying for her, and to my amazement is getting better. Their dramatic improvement cannot be explained scientifically...I have noticed also that the people who are nearing death, who have a strong faith in God and who are supported by prayer, have less anxiety and suffer less pain than those who do not have prayer support and strong belief.

Larry Dossey, M.D. wrote in his book, *Healing Words: The Power of Prayer and the Practice of Medicine*, about how while doing his residency at Parkland Memorial Hospital in Dallas, Texas, he encountered his first patient with a terminal case of cancer. The cancer had spread throughout both of the man's lungs. Dr. Dossey told him what treatments were available, but what little they could do. The man chose no treatment. And yet, whenever Dr. Dossey stopped by his hospital bedside, the man was surrounded by visitors from his church who were singing and praying.

A year later, when Dr. Dossey was working elsewhere, a colleague at Parkland called to ask if he wanted to see his old patient. Dr. Dossey writes,

> See him? I couldn't believe he was still alive. At the hospital I studied his chest x-rays. I was stunned. The man's lungs were completely clear. There was no sign of cancer.
> "His therapy has been remarkable," said the radiologist, looking over my shoulder. *Therapy?* I thought. *There wasn't any—unless you consider prayer.* I told two of my medical school professors what had happened. Neither of them were willing to acknowledge the man's miraculous healing. "That was the natural course of the disease," one said. The other professor shrugged. "We see this," he said. [2]

Dr. Dossey also made the following statements:

I had long given up the faith of my childhood. Now I believed in the power of modern medicine. Prayer seemed an arbitrary frill. So I put the incident out of my mind. The years passed and I became chief of staff at a large urban hospital. I was aware that many of my patients used prayer, but I put little trust in it. Then one day in the late 1980's I came across a study done by Randolph Byrd, a cardiologist at San Francisco General Hospital...I could not ignore the evidence...This study inspired me to look for others. To my amazement I found an enormous body of evidence: more than 100 experiments exhibiting the criteria of good science... Scientists, including physicians, can have blind spots. The power of prayer seemed to be one of them. [3]

Dr. Dossey has given up his practice of medicine and is devoting himself to writing and research about prayer and how it affects people's health. He has found that the power of prayer does not diminish with distance, and that *love* added to prayer increases its power.

Cardiologist Randolph Byrd reported in the *Southern Medical Journal* in 1986, that prayer can help heal people. Byrd's ten-month study of almost 400 patients in the coronary care unit at San Francisco General Hospital showed remarkable results.

The magazine, *Your Health,* in its April 5, 1994, issue, gives a summary of Byrd's rigid criteria, which mimicked typical medical clinical studies. Byrd's study was a randomized, double-blind experiment in which no one—not the patients, the nurses or doctors—knew which of two groups patients were in. One group of 192 patients was prayed for by home prayer groups, while the second group of 201 patients were not prayed for by these groups.

The people who prayed were given a brief description of each patient's diagnosis and condition, and each patient in the prayed-over group had between five and seven people praying for him.

Afterward, the study revealed these differences between the two groups:

- The patients who were prayed for were five times less likely to need antibiotics than those who were not.
- The prayed-for people were three times less likely to experience pulmonary edema (where the lungs fill with fluid because the heart is not pumping effectively) than the others.
- None of the 192 needed to be on mechanical ventilators, whereas twelve of the unprayed-for group required assistance in breathing.
- Fewer of the patients who were supported by prayer died.

Dossey felt that if the technique being studied had been a new drug or a surgical procedure instead of prayer, it would have been heralded as some sort of breakthrough.

In 1935, author Alexander Lake asked fifty physicians, chosen at random from the Los Angeles telephone directory, if they believed that spiritual healing–that is, physical and mental healings by faith alone—were possible.

Twenty-seven said, "Yes."
Eleven said, "I don't know."
Twelve said, "No."

Again in June 1955, he asked the same question of fifty Los Angeles doctors.

Forty-seven said, "Yes."
One said, "I don't know."
Two said, "No."

Three of the twelve who had said "No" in 1935 said "Yes" in 1955. When asked what had happened to change their minds, the three said, in effect, "We have learned that Man's natural state is one of well-being; and that there is a spiritual entity in Man that when activated by faith, destroys physical and mental illness." [4]

Later, because of a physical problem, Alexander Lake had surgery performed, and when he came out of anesthesia, he was vaguely aware that he was lying on a bed in a San Francisco veterans' hospital. Dr. Rab Lindsey, the surgeon who had operated, was bending over him. Alexander remembered that Dr. Lindsey had prayed before performing surgery, and so he asked him about it.

Dr. Lindsey told Alexander Lake his story. He was Scots-Canadian and had been raised on a forty-acre farm that his grandfather cleared in the forest. The days at home began with prayer and ended with prayer, with a short Bible reading before retiring for the night. During his growing-up years, Rab dreamed of becoming a doctor.

The time came when his father brought his *money-sock* from the battered, leather trunk in his bedroom, and while the family sat wide-eyed in a circle of lamplight, Father poured out on the table the savings of four years: $100.44. He put it into a homemade leather pouch, and handed it to Rab, telling him that the family was sending him off to college.

After college, he became a successful doctor. He was spoken of highly in medical circles, and he became self-assured, even smug and atheistic. However, after his third year of practice, there came a series of shocks. In one week, he lost two patients because of unforeseen complications following their operations. One afternoon the following week he looked up from his desk and saw what he thought must be a ghost. Nine months earlier, he had told a patient of his, Mr. Chapman, that he had no chance to live. Dr. Lindsey had told him that his malignancy had gone too far, and that surgery or nothing else could help him, but something happened. Dr. Lindsey described it this way:

Chapman grinned, "Fooled you, Doctor," he said. "Thought you should know that there was help for me." He pulled up a chair and sat down. "I've just had a check-up by a group of doctors," he said, "God—prayer has made me well."

I sat and stared at him. He went on: "You know, Doctor...the prayer of faith shall save the sick, and the Lord will raise him up..." [James 5:15].

"Tell me about it, Chapman," I said.

"Well, after I left here that day you pronounced my death sentence. I didn't *feel* like a condemned man. Instead, I felt anger against the evil trying to kill me.

I'd not really prayed for years, but that day as I walked the street, I found myself repeating a Bible verse I'd learned as a boy: *"Thou shalt not be afraid for the terror by night; nor for the arrow that flieth by day; Nor for the pestilence that walketh in darkness; nor for the destruction that wasteth at noonday"* [Psalm 91:5-6]. [5]

Mr. Chapman told Dr. Lindsey that he entered a church on the way home and on the pew where he sat there was a part of a pamphlet. It was a report by the Chicago Committee of the Commission on Religion and Health of the Federal Council of Churches. The committee consisted of Dr. Charles S. Braden, professor of History and Literature of Religions, Northwestern University; Dr. Carrol A. Wise of Garrett Biblical Institute; and Dr. W.E. Blakemore of the University of Chicago.

The report said that questionnaires had been sent to one thousand clergymen, and that those who had returned them had reported a total of 64 kinds of disease that had been cured by faith in God. There were several kinds of cancers: cancer of the lungs, the spine, the mouth, the duodenum, the bone, and in addition, ten unspecified kinds. The report said that in nearly every case, diagnosis had been made by a competent doctor, and there had been medical attendance for either a long or short period. Mr. Chapman continued:

> I read one case reported, over and over, Doctor. It was cancer, diagnosed and treated by a doctor who pronounced it hopeless of cure. Within one month, due

to prayer, that patient was well enough to go home. Within six months, she was doing her housework. Four years later, medical examination showed she was still completely healed. There were other kinds of spiritual healings reported: permanent cures of heart disease, paralysis, tuberculosis, polio, arthritis, and other ailments.

Well, Doctor, after I'd finished reading that report, I sat a long while, looking at a stained-glass window with the sunlight shining through it. I thought back over my life. I'd committed no crimes, but I'd been a hearty hater of those whom I'd thought had wronged me. I'd never taken revengeful *action* against any, but I'd cherished *thoughts* of revenge. Sitting there looking Death in the face, I realized my great sin was that the good I might have done, I'd left undone. "Forgive me, God, for having been one of Life's slackers," I said. At once, I experienced an inpouring of faith, and a surge of hope.

I don't really know how long I sat, recalling Bible texts I'd learned in Sunday school. And one I remembered with new understanding, strongly lifted my spirit: *"But unto you that fear my Name shall the Son of righteousness arise with healing in His wings"* [Malachi 4:2].

The sun was setting as I left the church. I then went to my own minister, and asked him to pray with me.

"That was almost nine months ago," he said. [6]

After this incident, Dr. Lindsey started seeking evidence of other miracles and did research with nine other doctors all in the same quest. When it was proven that there were miraculous healings, he was forced to accept the evidence. He shared with Alexander Lake the following words:

> The other nine doctors were happy to have proved that spiritual healings were possible, but I was dejected. I'd been compelled, by the evidence, to admit that God lived, and was able and willing to aid, comfort and heal. But that admission was not enough to lift the burden of guilt I felt because of my years of atheism. How many persons had I harmed, I wondered, by my ignorant assertions? [7]

Dr. Lindsey discussed his problem with Dr. Clyde Randolph, a minister versed in philosophy and literature, and he encouraged Dr. Lindsey to start reading the great scientists and psychologists. He read C.G. Jung, often called the greatest psychologist of all. He wrote,

> The truly religious person...knows that God has brought all sorts of strange and inconceivable things to pass, and seeks in the most curious ways to enter a man's heart. He therefore senses in everything the unseen presence of the divine will. [8]

Dr. Lindsey concluded that a little philosophy is indeed a dangerous thing. He said it made callow minds impudent, and on the other hand, profundity in philosophy invariably leads to God. For many years after this soul-searching experience, Dr. Lindsey had two quotations displayed on his office walls along with his diplomas. One had the words spoken by Dr. Amroise Pare, head army surgeon for Colonel Montejan about the year 1545, inscribed on it: *"I Dressed Them, and God Healed Them."* The word *dressed,* of course, meant "treated" or "operated."

The other plaque was inscribed with words by Alfred Lord Tennyson, from "Idylls of the King," as follows:

"Prayer"
More things are wrought by prayer
Than this world dreams of. Wherefore, let thy voice
Rise like a fountain for me night and day.
For what are men better than sheep or goats
That nourish a blind life within the brain
If, knowing God, they lift not hands of prayer
Both for themselves and those who call them friend?
For so the whole round earth is every way
Bound by gold chains about the feet of God. [9]

Dr. Alexis Carrell, a French surgeon and biologist, was born in Lyon, France, in 1873. He came to the United States in 1905, and was appointed to the Rockefeller Institute for Medical Research in 1906. He won the 1912 Nobel Prize in medicine for his work in blood vessel surgery and in transplanting organs and tissues. He wrote the following:

Prayer is not only worship; it is also an invisible emanation of man's worshipping spirit—the most powerful form of energy that one can generate. The influence of prayer on the human mind and body is as demonstrable as that of secreting glands. Its results can be measured in terms of increased physical buoyancy, greater intellectual vigor, moral stamina, and a deeper understanding of the realities underlying human relationships.

If you make a habit of sincere prayer, your life will be very noticeably and profoundly altered. Prayer stamps with its indelible mark our actions and demeanor. A tranquillity of bearing, a facial and bodily repose, are observed in those whose inner lives are thus enriched. Within the depths of consciousness a flame kindles. And man sees himself. He discovers his selfishness, his silly pride, his fears, his greeds, his blunders. He develops a sense of moral obligation, intellectual humility. Thus begins a journey of the soul toward the realm of grace.

Prayer is a force as real as terrestrial gravity. As a physician, I have seen men, after all other therapy has failed, lifted out of disease and melancholy by the serene effort of prayer. It is the only power in the world that seems to overcome the so-called "laws of nature;" the occasions on which prayer has dramatically done this have been termed "miracles." But a constant, quieter miracle takes place hourly in the hearts of men and women who have discovered that prayer supplies them with a steady flow of sustaining power in their daily lives.

Too many people regard prayer as a formalized routine of words, a refuge for weaklings, or a childish petition for material things. We sadly undervalue prayer when we conceive it in these terms, just as we should underestimate rain by describing it as something that fills the birdbath in our garden. Properly understood, prayer is a mature activity indispensable to the fullest development of personality—the ultimate integration of man's highest faculties. Only in prayer do we achieve that complete and harmonious assembly of body, mind, and spirit which gives the frail human reed its unshakable strength. [10]

Over forty years ago, author Dale Carnegie went with a friend who was suffering from an overactive thyroid to visit a doctor in Philadelphia. On the doctor's office wall hung a plaque painted with the following words:

Relaxing and Recreation
The most relaxing recreating forces are a healthy religion, sleep, music, and laughter.
Have faith in God. Learn to sleep well. Love good music, and see the funny side of life.
And health and happiness will be yours. [11]

Herbert Benson, M.D., author of several books and associate professor of medicine at Harvard Medical School and chief of the Section on Behavioral Medicine at New

England Deaconess Hospital, relates in his book, *Your Maximum Mind*, case after case of how people were helped by prayer to God and meditation, which strengthened their spiritual faith and belief for healing. Dr. Benson writes the following:

> The lives of Adam and Eve and their descendants are centered completely on how they relate to Yahweh, the faithful but demanding God who interacts constantly with them from their creation, through their fall, and on into their later acts of rebellion and obedience.
>
> This same spiritual saga continues today... According to surveys by the Gallup poll over the last few decades, a consistently high proportion of our population, about 95 percent, say that they believe in God. [12]

"Without Divine assistance I cannot succeed; with it I cannot fail."

Abraham Lincoln

CHAPTER 3

WHAT THE GREATS SAY ABOUT GOD AND PRAYER

Abraham Lincoln:
"I cannot conceive how a man could look up into the heavens and say there is no God." [1]
"I believe the Bible is the best gift God has ever given to man. All the good from the Saviour of the world is communicated to us through this book." [2]

George Washington:
"It is impossible to rightly govern the world without God and the Bible." [3]

Robert Lewis of Fredricksburg, Virginia, was Washington's private secretary. During the first part of the presidency, he said that he accidentally witnessed Washington's private devotions, both morning and evening. He saw him in a kneeling posture, with an open Bible before him; and he said that he believed such was his daily practice. His custom was to go to his library at four o'clock in the morning for devotions. [4]

John Quincy Adams:
"So great is my veneration of the Bible, that the earlier my children begin to read it the more confident will be my hope that they will prove useful citizens of their country and respectable members of society." [5]

Charles Dickens:
"The New Testament is the very best book that ever was or ever will be known in the world." [6]

Andrew Jackson:
"That book, sir, is the rock on which our republic rests." [7]

Horace Greeley:
"It is impossible to mentally or socially enslave a Bible-reading people. The principles of the Bible are the groundwork of human freedom." [8]

THE HEALING POWER OF PRAYER

Woodrow Wilson:
"I ask every man and woman in this audience that from this day on they will realize that part of the destiny of America lies in their daily perusal of this great Book." [9]

In the midst of President Wilson's difficulties in international negotiations he, too, felt the need of divine guidance. When Mr. Wilson arrived at a cabinet meeting his face wore a solemn look. It was evident that serious affairs of the nations were on his mind. He said to the cabinet members: "I don't know whether you men believe in prayer or not, I do. Let us pray and ask the help of God." The President of the United States fell upon his knees with the members of the cabinet, and offered a prayer to the Almighty for help. [10]

Douglas MacArthur:
"Believe me, sir, never a night goes by, be I ever so tired, but I read the Word of God before I go to bed." [11]

Dwight D. Eisenhower:
"To read the Bible is to take a trip to a fair land where the spirit is strengthened and faith renewed." [12]

Patrick Henry:
He was famous for his heroic exclamation: "Give me liberty or give me death!" Although he had an active and important role in forming the government of the United States he lacked business ability in the sense of

building up a personal fortune, so that at his death in 1799, his family was not surprised when they opened the will to read: "I have now disposed of all my property to my family. There is one thing more I wish I could give them and that is faith in Jesus Christ. If they had that and I had not given them one shilling, they would have been rich: and if they had not that, and I had given them all the world, they would be poor indeed." [13]

Shakespeare:
"I, William Shakespeare of Stratford-upon-Avon, in the country of Warrick, gentleman in perfect health and memory, God be praised, do make and ordain this my last will and testament in manner and form following, that is to say, first, I commend my soul into the hands of God, my Creator, hoping and assuredly believing, through the only merits of Jesus Christ, my Saviour, to be make partaker of life everlasting, and my body to the earth whereof it is made." [14]

Daniel Webster:
"...my heart has always assured and reassured me that the gospel of Jesus Christ must be a divine reality. The Sermon on the Mount cannot be a mere human production. This belief enters into the very depth of my conscience. The whole history of man proves it." [15]

"I believe Jesus Christ to be the Son of God. The miracles which he wrought establish, in my mind, his personal authority, and render it proper for me to believe whatever he asserts. I believe, therefore, all his declarations, as well when he declares himself to be the Son of God, as when he declares any other proposition." [16]

J. Pierpont Morgan:
This American financier and multi-millionaire formulated a 10,000-word will, which contained 37 articles. In it he inserted the following: "I commit my soul in the hands of my Saviour, full of confidence that, having redeemed me and washed me with His most precious Blood, He will present me faultless before the throne of my Heavenly Father.

"I entreat my children to maintain and defend, at all hazard and at any cost of personal sacrifice, the blessed doctrine of complete Atonement of sins through the Blood of Jesus Christ once offered, and through that alone." [17]

Thomas Jefferson (in one of his prayers):
"Almighty God, Who has given us this good land for our heritage; we humbly beseech Thee that we may always prove ourselves a people mindful of Thy favor and glad to do Thy will. Bless our land with honorable industry, sound learning, and pure manners.

"Save us from violence, discord, and confusion, from pride and arrogance, and from every evil way. Defend our liberties, and fashion into one united people the multitude brought hither out of many kindreds and tongues.

"Endow with the spirit of wisdom those to whom in Thy Name we entrust the authority of government, that there may be justice and peace at home, and that through obedience to Thy law, we may show forth Thy praise among the nations of the earth.

"In time of prosperity, fill our hearts with thankfulness, and, in the day of trouble, suffer not our trust in Thee to fail; all of which we ask through Jesus Christ our Lord. AMEN." [18]

Michelangelo:
"I die in the faith of Jesus Christ, and in the firm hope of a better life." [19]

Benjamin Franklin:
In 1787 the Constitutional Convention was on the verge of total failure over the issue of whether small states should have the same representation as large states. Benjamin Franklin, who was convinced that the Scripture was right when it stated, "Except the Lord build the house, they labor in vain that build it" [Psalm 127:1], asked the convention to pray.

He said, "Gentlemen, I have lived a long time and am convinced that God governs in the affairs of men. If a sparrow cannot fall to the ground without His notice, is it probable that an empire can rise without His aid? I move that prayer imploring the assistance of Heaven be held every morning before we proceed to business." [20]

The motion carried. The change after prayer was introduced was so dramatic that in a short while a compromise was reached which is still in effect today.

He also advocated having a Bible in every home. "A good newspaper and Bible in every home, a good schoolhouse in every district, and a church in every neighborhood, all appreciated as they deserve, are the chief support of virtue, morality, civil liberty and religion." [21]

John Harvard, president of Harvard University in the 1600's:
"Let every student be plainly instructed and earnestly pressed to consider well the main ends of his life and studies; to know God and Jesus Christ, which is eternal life, and therefore to lay Christ in the bottom as the only foundation of all knowledge and learning and see that the Lord only giveth wisdom. Let everyone seriously set himself by prayer in secret to see Christ as Lord and Master." [22]

Leo Tolstoy:
"I believe it is impossible to live well without prayer, and that prayer is the necessary condition of a good, peaceful, and happy life. The Gospels indicate how one should pray, and what prayer should consist of." [23]

Carl Sandberg:
To the thousands of students who wrote to Carl Sandberg asking him how to become a writer, Sandberg replied: "Solitude and prayer–then go on from there." [24]

Helen Keller:
"But how shall I speak of the glories I have since discovered in the Bible? For years I have read it with an ever-broadening sense of joy and inspiration; and I love it as I love no other book...The Bible gives me a deep, comforting sense the 'things seen are temporal, and things unseen are eternal.'" [25]

Emerson:
"No man ever prayed without learning something." [26]

St. Theresa of Avila:
    Let nothing disturb thee,
    Let nothing affright thee.
    All things are passing.
    God never changes.
    Patience gains all things.
    Who has God wants nothing.
    God along suffices. [27]

Francis de Sales:
"Do not look forward to the changes and chances of this life in fear; rather look to them with full hope that, as they arise, God, whose you are, will deliver you out of them. He has kept you hitherto—do you but hold fast to His dear hand, and He will lead you safely through all things; and, when you cannot stand, He will bear you in His arms. Do not look forward to what may happen tomorrow; the same everlasting Father who cares for you today will take care of you tomorrow, and every day. Ei-

ther He will shield you from suffering, or He will give you unfailing strength to bear it. Be at peace, then, and put aside all anxious thoughts and imaginations." [28]

> "The man without prayer…is as a city without walls, and open to all attacks."
>
> S. Chrysotom

CHAPTER 4

WHAT IS PRAYER AND HOW IMPORTANT IS IT?

Is prayer necessary? Does the Bible give direction to whom one should pray? Does God care about the problems of mankind? Is there help for mankind from divinity? Are prayers actually answered? The answer to all these questions is "yes."

> Prayer is the nearest approach to God, and the highest enjoyment of Him, that we are capable of in this life. It is the noblest exercise of the soul, the most exalted use of our best faculties and the highest imitation of the blessed inhabitants of Heaven. [1]

There is not in this world a kind of life more wonderful than a continual conversation with God and an awareness of His presence. When He is consulted before making a decision, not after; when He is thanked for everything; when He is looked upon as the Highest or Supreme authority; when He sits upon the throne of the heart, then there is true life, liberty, laughter, and light!

Although there is much discussion on prayer, there are many varied opinions to whom one should pray. Not only are there opinions, but there is much confusion and misconceptions about who or where God is. Sometimes people grow up confused wondering whom they should pray to and not really understanding God and the Bible. Writer Marty Kaplan shared in the June 24, 1996, issue of *Time* that he started out as a nice Jewish boy from Newark, New Jersey. He stated, "But with puberty came doubt, I became the Voltaire of Schuyler Avenue." After graduating from Harvard he felt as if he would spend his life as "a cultural Jew, an agnostic, a closet nihilist."

That all changed when he started suffering with a tooth-grinding problem. He started searching for help and found it this time in meditation. He wrote the following:

> The God I have found is common to Moses and Muhammad, to Buddha and Jesus. It is known to every mystic tradition. In mine, it is the Tetragrammaton, the Name so holy that those who know it dare not say it. It is what the Cabala calls Ayin, Nothingness, No-Thingness. It is Spirit, Being, the All.

I used to think of psychic phenomena a New Age flimflam. I used to think of reincarnation as a myth. I used to think the soul was a metaphor. Now I know there is a God–my God, in here, demanding not faith but experience, an inexhaustible wonder at the richness of this very moment. Now I know there is a consciousness that transcends science, a consciousness toward which our species is sputteringly evolving, a welcome development spurred ironically by our generational rendezvous with mortality.

People all over the earth are seeking truth just as Marty sought truth. There is only one truth that sets people free and brings them into contact with the one true God. Jesus stated that truth when He said, "I am the way, the truth, and the life: no man cometh unto the Father, but by me. If ye had known me, ye should have known my Father also: and from henceforth ye know him, and have seen him" (John 14:6-7). He also said, "The truth shall make you free" (John 8:32).

Many people become confused about who God is, to whom they should pray, and what prayer is. There must be a solid foundation of belief in the one true God. Confusion can come if the Holy Bible is not revered and obeyed, for it is the only thing that will stand. "The grass withereth, the flower fadeth: but the word of our God shall stand for ever" (Isaiah 40:8). The Holy Bible is the inspired Word of God, which makes it the highest authority on earth; therefore, it is the source from which one should seek information. "All scripture is given by inspiration of God" (II Timothy 3:16).

There are many doctrines and philosophies of men, religions that have *some* truth, and rituals that seek to bring man into a spiritual understanding of higher power. They cannot all be right. There are not many Gods; there is only one. "For thus saith the Lord that created the heavens; God himself that formed the earth and made it; he hath established it, he created it not in vain, he formed it to be inhabited: I am the Lord; and there is none else" (Isaiah 45:18).

To be able to pray effectively to this God, one must have faith that he is being heard by Him. Some say God does not demand faith but experience. Is this statement true? The only way to judge truth is to measure it against God's Word. Hebrews 11:6 refutes the statement that God does not demand faith, for He does. "But without faith it is impossible to please *him:* for he that cometh to God must believe that he is, and that he is a rewarder of them that diligently seek him."

To whom should one pray? Millions of people are not sure who Jesus is and look upon Him as being a prophet, a good teacher, or on the same level as Moses and other great Bible personalities. Jesus was more than that. He was God manifested in the flesh. I Timothy 3:16 says, "And without controversy great is the mystery of godliness: God was manifest in the flesh, justified in the Spirit, seen of angels, preached unto the Gentiles, believed on in the world, received up into glory." This describes Jesus. Jesus preached unto the Gentiles and was received up into glory. Jesus is not on the same level of Buddha, He is God who was manifested in the flesh. Buddha was just a man who lived and died, but Jesus lived, died for the sins of mankind, and rose on the third day and ascended to heaven. He became the mediator between God and man.

Jesus was the fulfillment of Isaiah 9:6 which says, "For unto us a child is born, unto us a son is given: and the government shall be upon his shoulder: and his name shall be called Wonderful, Counsellor, The mighty God, The everlasting Father, The Prince of Peace." The child was the mighty God manifest in the flesh.

John describes Jesus also. "In the beginning was the Word, and the Word was with God, and the Word was God...And the Word was made flesh, and dwelt among us..." (John 1:1,14).

Jesus had more than supernatural powers to heal the sick, the leper and the lame; He had the power to rebuke and cast devils out of people. He not only had the ability to be raised from the dead on the third day, but He stated in John 11:25, "I am the resurrection, and the life: he that believeth in me, though he were dead, yet shall he live."

Jesus gave hope when He spoke in Matthew 11:28, "Come unto me, all ye that labour, and are heavy laden, and I will give you rest." He also admonished the people as stated in Luke 18:1 to always pray and not to faint or give up. Hebrews 4:14-16 gives everyone the right to approach Him as an individual.

Seeing then that we have a great high priest, that is passed into the heavens, Jesus the Son of God, let us hold fast our profession. For we have not an high priest which cannot be touched with the feeling of our infirmities; but was in all points tempted like as we are, yet without sin. Let us therefore come boldly unto the throne of grace, that we may obtain mercy, and find grace to help in time of need.

Peter told the Sanhedrin after the lame man was healed at Gate Beautiful that the power they witnessed was not of man, but was in the name of Jesus, the one we are told to approach in prayer. Acts 4:10,12 says,

Be it known unto you all, and to all the people of Israel, that by the name of Jesus Christ of Nazareth, whom ye crucified, whom God raised from the dead, even by him doth this man stand here before you whole. Neither is there salvation in any other: for there is none other name under heaven given among men, whereby we must be saved.

It was Jesus who told His disciples and others to go into Jerusalem and wait in the upper room until they were endued with power from on high (Luke 24:49). As He was ascending into the heavens, He told them they would receive power after the Holy Ghost had come upon them (Acts 1:8).

How did this happen? They continued in prayer and supplications until there came a sound of a rushing mighty wind, and it filled the house and they were filled with the Holy Ghost and began to speak with other tongues, as the

Spirit spoke through them (Acts 1:14; 2:1-4). Prayer was the way they entered into His kingdom, and it is the way one stays there.

Jesus talked much about prayer while He walked upon earth because He wanted to save and help men and women of all generations and nationalities. He desired for people to incorporate prayer into their lifestyles, not just to use prayer for a time of crisis. This is shown in His answer to the disciples when they asked Him to teach them how to pray. He prayed the immortal prayer:

> Our Father which art in heaven, Hallowed be thy name. Thy kingdom come, Thy will be done in earth, as it is in heaven. Give us this day our daily bread. And forgive us our debts, as we forgive our debtors. And lead us not into temptation, but deliver us from evil: For thine is the kingdom, and the power, and the glory, for ever. Amen (Matthew 6:9-13).

It was a *daily* prayer.

Prayer is the language of the heart. Rote prayer is not real prayer. In the aforementioned *Newsweek* article, "Talking to God," Father Tilden Edwards, an Episcopal priest and executive director of Shalem Institute for Spiritual Formation in Washington, D.C., says when churches and synagogues rely on rote prayer, their liturgies "can be a way of evading God in the name of God."

How many people—even Christians—go through the motions of prayer to soothe their conscience or to further the tradition of past generations? How many *really* enjoy the time they spend in God's presence talking with Him? Many people are uncomfortable talking to God, about God or about prayer. Rabbi David Wolpe, a lecturer in Jewish Thought at the University of Judaism in Los Angeles, authored the book, *The Healer of Shattered Hearts: A Jewish View of God.* In it he wrote, "I stand up in front of Jewish groups and say, 'God loves you,' and watch them wince and squirm. We've so intellectualized the idea of prayer that we have bleached it of any emotional significance."

Yet the Holy Scriptures teach that fervent prayer is that which brings results. James 5:16 states, "Confess your faults one to another, and pray one for another, that ye may be healed. The effectual *fervent* prayer of a righteous man availeth much." To be fervent is to be passionate, intense, or to have great warmth or earnestness.

Prayer brings miracles and invokes the involvement of the Almighty God. Cecil Coffey shares an incredible story in the book, *God Ventures.* One day during the furious fighting on Okinawa in World War II, Desmond Doss stood beside a 77th Infantry Division lieutenant who was saying to his platoon, "Men, Doss is going to say a prayer before we go back on the lines. Doss, a shy-looking young medical aid man, stepped forward, removed his helmet, and in a soft Virginia drawl asked God's protection on the platoon.

Amazingly, the platoon came through that action without a single casualty. In a matter of minutes, word of the battlefield miracle flashed to the battalion commander and on to regimental and division levels. Hard-bitten colonels and generals pursed their lips in wonderment. Who was this praying medic anyway?

He was known as "The Preacher." He was classified as 1-A-O, which meant he was a conscientious objector who would serve in combat, but would not do combat. Everyone thought him odd because he did not wear a gun, but their opinion changed after they saw him in action. He performed so many feats of single-handed heroism that his name became a symbol for gallantry throughout the 77th division.

The most amazing feat of all occurred on April 29, 1945. When his company was ordered to assault a jagged escarpment ranging from 75 to 400 feet high, it was common knowledge that there would be heavy casualties, and the company commander, looking around, found only one medic aid man fit for action.

Before Doss went into battle, he stepped inside a foxhole to pray a few minutes and read his Bible. "As our troops gained the summit," the Army record reads, "a heavy concentration of artillery, mortar, and machine-gun fire crashed into them, inflicting approximately seventy-five casualties and driving the others back." [2]

The survivors regrouped, counted the missing and found that Doss was among them. Then someone shouted and pointed up. There, high above them, stood "The Preacher." He was waving frantically for a rope with which to lower the wounded. All about him were angry bursts of mortars and blasts of artillery.

The company commander ordered him down, but Doss refused, again signaling for a rope. There was nothing to do but help him. Meanwhile, the Japanese drew closer on the other side of the narrow summit. They started tossing grenades at Doss as he dashed here and there, tying tourniquets and giving plasma, and they made several attempts to overrun the top of the ridge, but were stopped by grenade barrages from Doss's buddies who had climbed back up to a ledge just under the escarpment crest.

For three sweating, concussion-rocked hours the slender medic tagged and hauled wounded men to the edge of the escarpment and lowered them—one by one—down the face of the cliff to friendly hands.

Five months later, the young medic stood on the lawn of the White House while President Truman placed the blue-ribboned Congressional Medal of Honor around his neck. For the first time in United States history, the nation had bestowed its highest military decoration on a conscientious objector. He preferred being called "conscientious cooperator."

Desmond Doss thanked his buddies for covering him while he worked all alone, but he knew he was not alone. God had sent angels to protect him from flying bullets and grenades, all because he honored God enough to pray and ask for help before entering into the battle.

While the world is crumbling and fear has paralyzed many hearts, let not fashion, materialism and superficial activity give false hope or take the place of that which is important, but let passionate prayers of repentance and intercession be uttered. It is imperative that people pray heaven-directed, earth-shaking prayers, so that we might be granted divine mercy and be delivered from the stagnation of apathy, while our generation trudges blindly into the blackness of violence and hell.

Leonard Ravenhill prayed the following heartfelt prayer:

> Lord, I tearfully ask:
> Teach me to pray with groanings so that there are earthquakes in hell.
> Teach me the groanings of the Spirit until angels stand in awe.
> Teach me Spirit-born intercession that changes history.
> Teach me the birth pangs of the Holy Ghost until hell-shaking revival is born.
> Lead me into travail that will hold back divine judgment from the nations for a little season. [3]

Ravenhill also described prayer and rebuked those who claim to be Christian and do not pray.

> "Prayer Is"
> Prayer is the most unexplored area of the Christian life.
> Prayer is the most powerful weapon of the Christian life.
> Prayer is the most hell-feared battle in the Christian life.
> Prayer is the most secret device of the Christian life.

Prayer is the most underestimated power in the Christian life.
Prayer is the most untaught truth in the Christian life.
Prayer is the most demanding exercise in the Christian life.
Prayer is the most neglected responsibility in the Christian life.
Prayer is the most conquering outreach in the Christian life.
Prayer is the most opposed warfare in the Christian life.
Prayer is the most far-reaching ministry in the Christian life. [4]

Andrew Bar David Urshan, known as an Apostle of Prayer, wrote the following:

Prayer is the great spiritual weapon with which we may all fight. It is not hampered by distance, and it is not limited by age or qualification. It links us to the source of unlimited and absolute power, and though all the forces of evil be arrayed against us, the victory is certainly ours. It is a wonderful privilege which we can never overstep, and which we dare not neglect. [5]

Read the following powerful metaphoric words spoken by the noble S. Chrysotom of the fourth century:

THE HEALING POWER OF PRAYER

Prayer is the medicine expelling spiritual sickness, the foundation of the spiritual building, that which the soul is to the body. The man without prayer is as the fish out of water, and gasping for life as a city without walls, and open to all attacks; but from him that is armed with prayer, the tempter starts back, as midnight robbers start back when they see a sword suspended over a soldier's bed. [6]

Ravenhill's prayer above, and these other writings are directed to people who have learned how to pray and intercede for nations and the needs of others. They possess hot hearts aflame with passion. These kinds of prayers are needful, but prayer to God takes on many forms. It is not just asking and interceding, but it is also praise, adoration and thanksgiving. It is communing with Him alone.

Prayer is giving God undivided attention, closing out all others. Prayer takes the edges off; it lubricates the soul. Prayer lets a person see into the realm of the spirit world; it takes your eyes off the tangibles and allows you to see beyond.

In *None of These Diseases,* psychiatrist William Sadler said the following about prayer:

Prayer is a powerful and effectual worry-remover. Men and women who have learned to pray with child-like sincerity, literally talking to, and communing with the Heavenly Father, are in possession of the great secret whereby they can cast their care upon God, knowing that He careth for us.

Many are victims of fear and worry because they fail properly to maintain their spiritual nutrition...The majority of people liberally feed their bodies, and many make generous provision for their mental nourishment; but the vast leave the soul to starve, paying very little attention to their spiritual nutrition; and as a result the spiritual nature is so weakened that it is unable to exercise the restraining influence over the mind which would enable it to surmount its difficulties and maintain an atmosphere above conflict and despondency. [7]

Prayer not only brings people out of despondency but it helps strengthens marriages. The *Newsweek* article, "Talking to God," states that sociologist Andrew M. Greeley's studies show that spouses who pray together report greater marital satisfaction than those who don't. When there has been no prayer, and marriages fall into great disarray, God still listens to prayers from couples or a spouse whose heart is broken. "The Lord is nigh unto them that are of a broken heart; and saveth such as be of a contrite spirit" (Psalm 34:18).

God does want to help people but He desires for them to communicate with Him in their times of troubles. Author Evelyn Christenson, who wrote the book *What happens When Women Pray?*, believes that prayer is one of God's chief means of accomplishing His will on earth.

The question asked in the beginning paragraph, "Does God care about the problems of mankind?" could be answered many ways. Let the story of Captain Eddie Rickenbacker answer this. During World War II the plane he was on had been forced down into the Pacific Ocean. For eight days he and his friends had been drifting helplessly, without food or water, in the scorching tropic sun. The heat, hunger and exhaustion had brought them close to the breaking point.

But not Captain Rickenbacker, for he believed in prayer. He had learned to pray as a child at his mother's knee; and in all the crises of his life, prayer had given him comfort and courage. On the eighth day he read from Matthew the following passage:

> Therefore take no thought saying, What shall we eat? or, What shall we drink? or, Wherewithal shall we be clothed?...for your heavenly Father knoweth that ye have need of these things.
> But seek ye first the kingdom of God, and His righteousness; and all these things shall be added unto you.
> Take therefore no thought for the morrow; for the morrow shall take thought for the things of itself. Sufficient unto the day is the evil thereof (Matthew 6:31-34). [8]

Captain Rickenbacker wrote the following words after their rescue:

> We saw nothing in the way of searching planes or ships. The boy in my boat had an issue Bible in the pocket of his jumper, and the second day out we organ-

ized little evening and morning prayer meetings and took turns about reading passages from the Bible. Frankly and humbly we prayed for our deliverance. After the oranges were gone, we experienced terrific pangs of hunger, and we prayed for food.

We had a couple of little fish lines with hooks about the size of the end of my little finger, but no bait. Were it not for the fact that I have seven witnesses, I wouldn't dare tell this story because it seems so fantastic. Within an hour after prayer meeting on the eighth day, a sea gull came out of nowhere and landed on my head. I reached up my hand very gently and got him. We wrung his head, feathered him, carved up his carcass and ate every bit, even the little bones. We distributed and used his innards for bait.

Captain Cherry caught a little mackerel about six or eight inches long and I caught a little speckled sea bass about the same size, so we had food for a couple of days....

That night we ran into our first rainstorm. Usually you try to avoid a black squall, but in this case we made it our business to get into it and catch water for drinking...Later we were able to catch more water and build up our supply. [9]

The day this story appeared in the newspapers, people everywhere were noticeably affected by it...It was an amazing demonstration of the power of prayer...Every paper in the land picked up Rickenbacker's story... People who hadn't prayed in years began to do so again. Some who had never prayed in their lives began to search their souls with a new questioning. Many who were anguished, bitter, and despairing, who had suffered profound grief during the war, felt the pain of their hearts ease and the bitterness leave them. It was as though something wonderful and fine had happened to everyone, everywhere...as indeed it had! [10]

"I consider the story of how we prayed and how our prayers were answered the most important message I ever gave to the people of this country," wrote Captain Rickenbacker. [11]

Prayer lets a person enter into the spirit world, for God is a Spirit. Prayer knows no distance or limitations. Prayer and answers to prayer can cross prison lines, boundaries of different countries and even spin through space until they reach the throne of God. This happened with Daniel of old. When he prayed, a prince of hell tried to hold the answer to his prayer from coming back to the earth, but a heavenly angel fought the prince and the answer was delivered to Daniel.

Prayer is not a hard thing to do, it is just a matter of making it a priority. It is simply letting the heart reach out to God and talking to Him boldly as Hebrews 4:16 says to do. "Let us therefore come boldly unto the throne of grace, that we may obtain mercy, and find grace to help in time of need."

David Clarkson wrote,

> The word *boldly* signifies liberty without restraint. You may be free, for you are welcome. You may use freedom of speech... You have liberty to speak your minds freely, to speak all your heart, your ails, and wants, and fears, and grievances. As others may not fetter you in speaking to God by prescribing what words you should use; so you need not restrain yourselves, but freely speak all that your condition requires. [12]

> Prayer is so simple;
> It is like quietly opening a door
> And slipping into the very presence of God,
> There in the stillness
> To listen to His voice;
> Perhaps to petition,
> Or only to listen;
> It matters not.
> Just to be there
> In his presence
> Is prayer. [13]

Dr. Alexis Carrel asked the question in his article *Prayer is Power*, written in 1941, "How can prayer be defined?" The answer is found in the following words:

> Prayer is the effort of man to reach God, to commune with an invisible being, creator of all things, supreme wisdom, truth, beauty, and strength, father and redeemer of each man. [14]

Prayer is simply having a visit with God in His throne room. To literally feel God's presence and Spirit when sincere prayer is made to Him is the most incredible, ecstatic experience, for in His presence is fullness of peace, joy and true love.

"The sovereign cure for worry is prayer."

William James

CHAPTER 5

THE HEALING POWER OF PRAYER FOR THE MIND

Unique is the mind and powerful is its ability. The mind has the capability to remember and to affect thinking; it is the inner world of thought. It is the subject of consciousness; that which feels, perceives, wills and thinks. It is affected by emotions, experiences, and encounters with factual material.

The mind can become overloaded with stress, negative information, and the effects of bad experiences which can result in a breakdown or sense of despair. When a healing is needed there is nothing that will help heal the mind more quickly than being able to pray to God and asking Him for help.

Four hundred years ago Francis Bacon said, "A little philosophy inclineth man's mind to atheism; but depth in philosophy bringeth men's minds about to religion." [1] Dale Carnegie wrote,

> I can remember the days when people talked about the conflict between science and religion. But no more. The newest of all sciences, psychiatry, is teaching what Jesus taught. Why? Because psychiatrists realize prayer and a strong religious faith will banish the worries, the anxieties, the strains and fears that cause more than half of all our ills. Dr. A.A. Brill said: "Anyone who is truly religious does not develop a neurosis." [2]

The January 21, 1996, issue of the *Contra Costa Times* newspaper carried an article entitled, "Scientists Examine the Healing Powers of Prayer," written by John Boudreau. In the article, James Billings, senior vice president of the Preventive Medicine Research Institute in Sausalito, says,

> People assumed thoughts are free: that as long as you only think things, it was no big deal. Now we know if we think it, our body experiences it. Stress, worry, fear—all of that has an effect on our physiology. If you visualize a frightening experience, your body responds to that visualization.

Dale Carnegie interviewed Henry Ford a few years prior to his death, and expected to find a man who showed the strains of the long years he had spent in building up and managing one of the world's greatest businesses. Instead of finding a man with a frazzled mind, Mr. Carnegie was surprised to find Ford calm, well and peaceful-looking at age 78. When Mr. Carnegie asked him if he ever worried, he replied, "No. I believe God is managing affairs and that He doesn't need any advice from me. With God in charge, I believe that everything will work out for the best in the end. So what is there to worry about?" [3]

Dr. O.F. Gober, one of the medical executives of the Santa Fe Railway back in the 1940's, and whose official title was chief physician of the Gulf, Colorado and Santa Fe Hospital Association, said,

> Seventy per cent of all patients who come to physicians could cure themselves if they only got rid of their fears and worries. Don't think for a moment that I mean that their ills are imaginary. Their ills are as real as a throbbing toothache and sometimes a hundred times more serious. I refer to such illnesses as nervous indigestion, some stomach ulcers, heart disturbances, insomnia, some headaches, and some types of paralysis...These illnesses are real. I know what I am talking about, for I myself suffered from a stomach ulcer for twelve years.
> Fear causes worry. Worry makes you tense and nervous and affects the nerves of your stomach and actually changes the gastric juices of your stomach from normal to abnormal and often leads to stomach ulcers. [4]

There are many kinds of fear which cause the mind to be filled with anxiety and worry. Fear, caused by many factors, brings agony and distress to an already disturbed mind. Man was not made to house a fearful mind; he was made to have a sound mind, full of power. "For God hath not given us the spirit of fear; but of power, and of love, and of a sound mind" (I Timothy 1:7).

The book, *Theory and Practice of Psychiatry,* published in 1936, attests that prayer helped heal a lady with mental and emotional problems. Dr. Lena Sadler had asked her husband, Dr. William S. Sadler, to see one of her patients, a refined, highly-educated woman. The patient still did not respond, even after their combined psychiatric counselings. Dr. William Sadler advised his wife that she need not expect any worthwhile improvement until her patient's mental life was set in order and numerous psychic slivers were removed. To the question of how long he thought that would take, he replied that it would take probably a year or more.

Dr. William Sadler tells in his own words what happened:

> Imagine my surprise when this patient walked into my office a few days later and informed me that her "troubles were over," and the things she had assured me a few days previously she "could never do," had all been done, that everything I had asked her to do as part of her "cure" had been set in operation. She had completely overhauled her social, family, and personal life, had made numerous "confessions," and had accom-

plished a score of almost impossible mental and "moral" stunts.

In reply to my astonished question, "How in the world did you ever do all this and effect this great change in your mental attitude toward yourself and the world in less than one week?" she smilingly replied, "Dr. Lena taught me to pray." [5]

Plato said, "The greatest mistake physicians make is that they attempt to cure the body without attempting to cure the mind; yet the mind and body are one and should not be treated separately." [6]

Herbert Benson, M.D., stated in his book, *Your Maximum Mind*, that the mind can be healed or altered by prayer, meditation and faith.

The Relaxation Response has been the focal point of my own medical research and clinical practice for the last twenty years. For those of you who are unfamiliar with this work, the Relaxation Response refers to the ability of the body to enter into a scientifically definable state characterized by an overall reduction of the speed of the body's metabolism, lowered blood pressure, decreased rate of breathing, lowered heart rate, and more prominent, slower brain waves.

The Relaxation Response has its most powerful impact when combined with what I've called the Faith Factor. This involves eliciting the Response in the context of a deeply held set of personal, religious or philosophical beliefs. [7]

Dr. Benson further explains that,

> Over the years, you develop "circuits" and "channels" of thought in your brain. These are physical pathways which control the way you think, the way you act, and often, the way you feel. Many times, these pathways or habits become so fixed that they turn into what I call "wiring." In other words, the circuits or channels become so deeply ingrained that it seems almost impossible to transform them. They actually become part of your brain; they are part of you.
>
> In very practical terms, then, it's largely the established circuits of the left side of our brain that are telling us, "You can't change your way of living...Your bad habits are forever...You're just made in a certain way, and you have to live with that fact."
>
> That simply is not true. Significant, even dramatic change is possible. How? By eliciting the Relaxation Response through meditation, prayer or other techniques, you can set the stage for important mind-and habit-altering brain change.
>
> Scientific research has shown that electrical activity between the left and right sides of the brain becomes coordinated during certain kinds of meditation or prayer. [8]

Scientists have wondered, discussed and researched the controversial subject of whether the brain is the same as the mind. Dr. Benson brings this to our attention, and also explains what thoughts are and how they interact with the body. He writes the following:

> Among other things, a healthy brain cell stores and transmits information which ultimately becomes what we know as *thoughts*. It's very difficult to describe exactly what happens in this process because the whole act of thinking is so complex, with enormous numbers of brain cells interacting in our mental processes. Consider, for instance, that there are approximately 100 *billion* nerve cells in your brain.
>
> Moreover, when you look closely at the makeup of each one of the 100 billion nerve cells, the whole matter gets indescribably more complicated. Each of the nerve cells has numerous tentacles, or axons and dendrites. During brain activity, these "communicate" with the tentacles of other cells through connections called synapses; thereby the brain cells interact and do their work. Dendrites also communicate with other parts of their own cell. [9]
>
> Is the mind the same as the brain?...There's been considerable discussion about this point over the years. Some argue that our minds are the sum total of our brain's physical capabilities, nothing more and nothing less. But Sir John Eccles, who won the Nobel Prize for Medicine in 1963, has rejected such a mechanistic view of man's thinking processes. He doesn't think that the power of the mind rests exclusively in nerve cells, dendrites, synapses and neurotransmitters.

Rather, he states, "I believe that there is a fundamental mystery in my existence, transcending any biological account of the development of my body (including my brain) with its genetic inheritance and its evolutionary origin."

Eccles goes on to argue, "If I say that the uniqueness of the human self is not derived from experiment, then what is it derived from? My answer is this: from a divine creation. Each self is a divine creation."

In a similar vein, the famous Canadian neurosurgeon Wilder Penfield wrote in *The Mystery of the Mind* that the workings of the mind will probably always be impossible to explain simply on the basis of electrical or chemical action in the brain and nervous system.

"The mind is independent of the brain," he declared. "The brain is a computer, but it is programmed by something that is outside itself, the mind." [10]

Webster's Dictionary gives several definitions of the mind. The third definition states that the mind is that from which thought originates. It is the subject of consciousness: that which feels, perceives, and thinks.

Wisdom of Old states that a man is what he thinks. "For as he thinketh in his heart, so is he" (Proverbs 23:7).

There are thousands of people that develop neurosis when life seems to hand them a *bad* deal. This happened to a woman named Gail. Dr. Benson tells about her in his book, *Your Maximum Mind*.

Gail had many things happen in her life that caused her to be on a downward course, but one good thing she had in all her troubles was a seed of faith planted in her early in childhood. As she withdrew from the company of people, she began to spend long hours alone. In the past, when her life had been filled with family and work concerns, she had given little time to prayer and meditation. Now, with nowhere else to turn but her religion, she began to spend long periods, sometimes an hour or more, in prayer and meditation. She began reading her Bible and self-help books daily.

Without being at all aware of what she was doing, Gail thus began to reprogram her way of thinking along more positive and productive lines. As she alternated between her prayers, the self-help books and the Bible, she soon found that her outlook on life brightened considerably. [11]

Dr. Benson also shares the story of Mike, who developed a severe case of claustrophobia. Dr. Benson gave Mike the following steps, and they helped Mike overcome his problem:
- Pray to ask God to help you overcome this problem.
- Then meditate on a passage of Scripture–preferably one that is meaningful to you, but not necessarily one connected with the claustrophobia.
- After fifteen or twenty minutes of this meditation, ask God to draw your eye to another passage of Scripture which may somehow be related to good health or even

to this problem of claustrophobia. When you find the passage, focus on it; think about it deeply; and try to see practical ways that it may apply to the problem you're facing.
- When you find yourself in another closed-in situation, imagine that Jesus Himself is right there with you, comforting you and supporting you.

Mike was a little skeptical because he had never tried praying and meditating in quite this way before...He chose the meditative phrase "God is Love," from the first epistle of John. Then, as he began to look through some of his favorite Biblical passages to use after the twenty-minute period of meditation, he settled upon a section of Psalm 139: "Where can I go from thy spirit? Or where can I flee from my presence?...If I take the wings of the dawn, if I dwell in the remotest part of the sea, even there thy hand will lead me, and thy right hand will lay hold of me" (Psalm 139:7,9-10).

Mike's recovery turned out to be rather rapid. He did experience a few twinges of anxiety as he entered the car and then moved into the elevator. But he had prepared well...Mike continued to practice these same techniques for a number of weeks. [12]

The reason this meditation and prayer worked for Mike and Gail is because it is founded upon truths penned nearly 2,000 years ago, but that are still effective today. The truth of the Word is this:

For the word of God is quick, and powerful, and sharper than any twoedged sword, piercing even to the dividing asunder of soul and spirit, and of the joints and marrow, and is a discerner of the thoughts and intents of the heart (Hebrews 4:12).

The truth of prayer spoken by Jesus is this: "Men ought always to pray, and not to faint" (Luke 18:1). When you link both prayer to God and meditation of His Word together, you have an unbeatable combination that guarantees health, success, happiness and a sound mind.

The *Newsweek* article, "Talking to God," includes a statement by psychiatrist Arthur Kornhaber, who works with troubled adolescents. He says it well: "To exclude God from psychiatric consultation is a form of malpractice. Spirituality is wonder [and] joy, and shouldn't be left in the clinical closet."

Poet Richard Trench sums it up well in the following poem:

> "Prayer"
> Lord, what a change within us one short hour
> Spent in thy presence will prevail to make!
> What parched grounds refresh as with a shower!
> We kneel, and all around us seems to lower;
> We rise, and all, the distant and the near,
> Stands forth in sunny outline brave and clear;
> We kneel, how weak! we rise, how full of power!
> Why, therefore, should we do ourselves this wrong,
> Or others, that we are not always strong,

That we are ever overborne with care,
That we should ever weak or heartless be,
Anxious or troubled, when with us is prayer,
And joy and strength and courage are with thee! [13]

When anyone is in trouble and hurting emotionally, they should cry out to God for help. St. Augustine said it this way: "How deep in the deep are they who do not cry out of the deep." [14]

> "I am the Lord that healeth thee."
>
> Exodus 15:26

CHAPTER 6

THE HEALING POWER OF PRAYER FOR THE BODY

On April 14, 1902, a young man with $500.00 in cash opened a dry goods store in Kemmerer, Wyoming. Kemmerer was a little mining town of a thousand people, situated on the old covered-wagon trail laid out by the Lewis and Clark Expedition. The young man and his wife lived in a half-story attic above the store, using boxes for a table and chairs.

Today, one of the largest chain of drygoods stores in the world bears that man's name: J.C. Penney.

Dale Carnegie, author of *How to Stop Worrying and Start Living,* had lunch with Mr. Penney, and Penney related to him one of the most dramatic moments of his life. These were his words:

Years ago, I passed through a most trying experience. I was worried and desperate. My worries were not connected in any way whatever with the J.C. Penney Company. That business was solid and thriving; but I personally had made some unwise commitments prior to the crash of 1929. Like many other men, I was blamed for conditions for which I was in no way responsible. I was so harassed with worries that I couldn't sleep, and developed an extremely painful ailment know as the shingles, a red rash and skin eruptions. I consulted a physician, a man with whom I had gone to high school as a boy in Hamilton, Missouri: Dr. Elmer Eggleston, a staff physician at the Kellogg Sanitarium in Battle Creek, Michigan. Dr. Eggleston put me to bed and warned me that I was a very ill man. A rigid treatment was prescribed. But nothing helped. I got weaker day by day. I was broken nervously and physically, filled with despair, unable to see even a ray of hope. I had nothing to live for. I felt I hadn't a friend left in the world, that even my family had turned against me. One night, Dr. Eggleston gave me a sedative, but the effect soon wore off and I awoke with an overwhelming conviction that this was my last night of life. Getting out of bed, I wrote farewell letters to my wife and to my son, saying that I did not expect to live to see the dawn.

When I awoke the next morning, I was surprised to find that I was still alive. Going downstairs, I heard singing in a little chapel where devotional exercises were held each morning. I can still remember the hymn they were singing: "God will take care of you." Going into the chapel, I listened with a weary heart to the singing, the reading of the Scripture lesson, and the prayer. Suddenly, something happened. I can't explain it. I can only call it a miracle. I felt as if I had been instantly lifted out of the darkness of a dungeon into warm, brilliant sunshine. I felt as I had been transported from hell to paradise. I felt the power of God as I had never felt it before. I realized then that I alone was responsible for my troubles. I knew that God with His love was there to help me. From that day to this, my life has been free from worry. I am seventy-one years old, and the most dramatic and glorious twenty minutes of my life were those I spent in that chapel that morning: "God will take care of you." [1]

Christ suffered for humanity and died a humiliating death so that all could have salvation. Not only was His suffering for salvation, but it was also for healing. Peter, in describing Christ's sufferings, added this truth: "...by whose stripes ye were healed" (I Peter 2:24). This truth substantiates Psalm 103:2-3: "Bless the Lord, O my soul, and forget not all his benefits: Who forgiveth all thine iniquities; who *healeth all thy diseases.*"

In order for some healings to take place, there must be a release by the patient of things that are bothering him: any resentments or negative, tense emotions. Dr. William Sadler ascertained that a clear conscience is a great step toward barricading the mind against neuroticism and the body against disease. He wrote,

No one can appreciate so fully as a doctor the amazingly large percentage of human disease and suffering which is directly traceable to worry, fear, conflict, immorality, dissipation, and ignorance—to unwholesome thinking and unclean living. *The sincere acceptance of the principles and teachings of Christ with respect to the life of mental peace and joy, the life of unselfish thought and clean living, would at once wipe out more than half the difficulties, diseases, and sorrows of the human race.* In other words, more than one half of the present affliction of mankind could be prevented by the tremendous prophylactic power of actually living up to the personal and practical spirit of the real teachings of Christ. [2]

Dr. Robert Ornstein, psychologist, brain researcher and writer, and Dr. David Sobel, regional director of preventive medicine for Kaiser Permanente, wrote the following in their book, *Healthy Pleasures:*

You are probably quite familiar with the claim that confession is good for the soul. But confession is more than a moral issue: it can sometimes be good for the body as well...In the mind, a covered over negative event is never finished. People tend to mull over the trauma again and again in their mind; rehearsing what they should have said, what they might have done. Writing about something or confiding in someone may force you to organize your thoughts and feelings about events, revealing hidden biases and unresolved issues.

THE HEALING POWER OF PRAYER

Once it is "out there," you can often distance yourself from the traumatic experience. By "getting it off your chest," you may be able to break the endless recycling of negative thoughts and feelings. This may be one of the reasons why many religious traditions, and self-help groups encourage confession... The act of confession may well enable a person to improve his or her health. [3]

Authors Caryle Hirshberg and Marc Ian Barasch relate several incidents of miraculous healings in their book, *Remarkable Recovery*. In early 1982, Carol Knudtson, 52, developed a fast-growing lymphoma on her neck. "The report on her case in the journal *Cancer* describes Carol's disease as an 'aggressive histologic subtype' in which regression is extremely rare." [4]

Yet, in Carol's case, the cervical lymph node regressed completely and the physical exam was completely normal by late spring 1982. In less than six weeks, every symptom of cancer was completely gone!

What happened? According to Carol, it was a combination of prayer and positive thinking. As a child, she had always been something of a fanatic, diligently clipping out Norman Vincent Peale columns from the daily paper. Religion, too, had been a vital force in her life ever since she had gone to Bible school. In her home, the radio is tuned constantly to a religious station. During the illness, she felt strengthened by the fact that her mother, sister, sister-in-law, and a church "prayer-chain" had implored God for her cure.

WHAT IS PRAYER AND HOW IMPORTANT IS IT?

When Christine Anderson developed breast cancer, she went through the cancer process: mammogram, biopsy, mastectomy and chemotherapy. Her second treatment caused convulsions and an alarming plummet in blood pressure that had required a transfusion. Then, the bad news. Lung metastases were discovered, their spread and size too advanced for surgery. The physicians gave her three months to live and gently suggested she not delay in making out her will.

Christine related that church had always been a central part of her life. One Sunday, she heard a doctor give a testimony about his heart disease and receive anointment with holy oil.

She decided that if a doctor could ask for divine aid, she too wanted to be anointed, embraced by the community of believers. All that month, every day, she wrote over and over in her diary her simple affirmations: "I know God can heal me...I know that God heals...with You watching over me...." [5]

On her next checkup, amazingly, her lungs were clear. Not long after, her glossy, dark brown hair grew back in...Today, five years later, Christine's lungs remain cloudless. "I don't call it spontaneous remission," she insists, "I call it divine intervention." [6]

Dr. Scott, asked by a local journalist if he would class Christine a miracle, answered, "I wouldn't argue against it." [7]

THE HEALING POWER OF PRAYER

When Rita McLaughlin developed multiple sclerosis, the disease progressed rapidly. The MS caused complete paralysis of both feet and ankles, and she was confined most of the time to a wheelchair, wearing sometimes the full-length steel leg braces and forearm crutches. She felt bitter at God and hated herself and everybody around her. Finally one day, her husband asked her to attend a healing service.

While at the service, with the people waving their hands and saying, "Hallelujah," and the minister praying over her, she said her bitterness gave way to:

> ...the strangest experience. I didn't see the people anymore... There was just this white light, a feeling of absolute love like I'd never felt coursing through me. I felt forgiven and at peace. I wasn't physically healed, but had peace of heart, of knowing I was loved and could weather anything. [8]

The disease continued its progress, and the doctors told her there was no hope of improvement. The damage to nerves and tissues was irreversible. But she writes,

> I went back to my life of prayer, but one based not on books or scriptures or tradition but a personal relationship with Jesus. It was a more mature faith, a working faith: I stopped thinking about myself first all the time. I started looking at people who were worse off in a thousand different ways, if not with disease then with family problems, alcoholism, drugs, depression. I

couldn't help them physically, but at least I could be supportive, listen to them, and pray. [9]

Six months later, Rita heard a voice saying, "Why don't you ask?" She felt a prayer rising within her asking for faith that would move mountains. She instantly felt "a sudden surge of electricity down the back of my neck and into my arms and legs...pins-and-needles...a sparkling feeling of effervescence...It went through the right side of my body, which was most affected." [10]

The next morning she noticed "a rush of heat that was like fire, starting at my feet and roaring up through my body."

The next thing she knew, her legs began to itch unbearably. She bent over to scratch at the heavy cotton stockings she wore to keep her braces from rubbing sores on her skin and realized she had sensation in the lower part of her legs. More shockingly, "I could wiggle my toes, something I had not been able to do for over ten years." [11]

When she arrived home, she looked at the kneecap, which since the tendons had been cut had been deformed, facing sideways, and it looked as if it was back in place. She screamed, "I'm healed! I'm healed!" She ran up the stairs, down the stairs, and outside shouting to the sky her thanksgiving.

When she went to her doctors for examination, they were flabbergasted. She said her neurologist was very angry, saying that there was no cure for MS, and no such thing as miracles, but her urologist, who had last seen her with her bladder swollen to many times its normal size and incontinent, retested her and confirmed that the organ had returned to normal. "He said there was no way he could explain it, that it was the most beautiful thing he'd ever seen in all his years of practice, and then he cried." [12]

Not everyone was overjoyed at Rita's miracle. There were those who could not deal with anything that could not be proven scientifically. But God, who created science, the world, atoms and all matter, has the power to do anything He chooses to do. He would like to do more good things for more people, but there must first be *belief*. This simple truth is contained in the words Jesus spoke to the multitudes when He walked the earth. He said, "Be not afraid, only believe" (Mark 5:36).

In the already-mentioned *Contra Costa Times* article by John Boudreau, "Scientists Examine the Healing Powers of Prayer," he reports that in December 1995, Harvard Medical School held a conference on the topic, "Spirituality & Healing in Medicine." Dr. Dale Matthews, an internist at Georgetown University Hospital in Washington, D.C., who spoke at the conference, said, "Faith in general is good for your health. We have over 200 studies indicating that's true."

Included also in the article is the statement made by Dr. David B. Larson, a psychiatrist and epidemiologist and former senior researcher for the National Institutes of Health and who now directs the private National Institute for Healthcare Research in Rockville, Maryland, which studies the relationship between spirituality and mental and physical health. He said,

> Statistically, God is good for you. I'm a psychiatrist. I was told by my professors that religion is harmful. Then I looked at the research, and religion is actually highly beneficial. If you go to church or pray regularly, it's very beneficial in terms of preventing illness, mental and physical, and you cope with illness much more effectively. If you look at the research, in area after area, it's 80 percent beneficial. I was shocked.

In the same article are several examples of answers to prayer. Marty Riser, who was suffering from myocarditis, a rare infection that caused his heart to enlarge and malfunction, was placed on the "A" list to get a new heart at Stanford Medical Center. When it arrived, Marty and his wife prayed together before the operation, and he was very positive that he was in the hands of God. More than six years later, he is working full-time and enjoying watching his son and daughter enter adulthood.

Mr. Boudreau also relates the story of Larry Eason. The doctors gave him six months to live when he was diagnosed with a malignant lung tumor. Two years later, he is still alive. Larry and Beverly Eason are certain that prayer support from their church played a crucial role. They said,

> We look at it as a miracle...There's no doubt in my mind that prayer helped him. Absolutely. I'm not say-

ing the medical people didn't help. Imagine a cake with no frosting. Prayer is the frosting on the cake. They enhance each other.

Mr. Boudreau writes, "Academics and medical doctors say research indicates this: People who are religious appear to live healthier lives than those who aren't religious. They are less susceptible to diseases such as cancer and cardiovascular conditions."

I received a call from a friend, Linda Gonzales, who had advanced asthma. She had been taking four kinds of medication a day. She said she was sitting in a church service and there was a man who was praying for the sick who called her out of the crowd and prayed for her. When he commanded the asthma to leave her body, she said she was healed instantly. She was rejoicing over her newfound health—no more inhalers, wheezing or medication. She was set free and tells everyone that it was a miracle from God.

Charles Kettering, the famous research scientist, is impatient with people who speak of insurmountable obstacles. "It is like the doctors with their incurable diseases," he says. "Did you ever stop to think what an incurable disease is? It is one the doctor doesn't know how to cure." [13]

Robert Jordan tells about receiving a telephone call from his wife who was distraught: a truck had run over their 22-month-old baby, Samantha, and she suffered severe head injuries. After hearing the terrible news, he ran out of the factory where he was working, jumped in his car, and raced to the hospital in Amory, Mississippi. When he arrived at the hospital, Samantha was not moving, her eyes did not blink; she had no response at all. The local doctors were doing all they could while waiting for a helicopter to arrive from the nearby town of Tupelo that would carry her to Lebonheur Children's Hospital in Memphis, Tennessee.

About two-and-one-half hours later Robert and his wife arrived in Memphis where Samantha had been admitted to the Intensive Care Unit. The doctor informed them that Samantha's skull was fractured in four places, but they were not sure how much damage was done to the brain. There was nothing to do but wait and see.

After four days Samantha's condition was unchanged. She was still unconscious and not responding at all. The doctors gave very little hope for her. A CAT scan was done, and x-rays showed that the right side of her brain was heavily damaged. In addition, she began having seizures. Things were not looking good at all.

Robert wrote,

> Although I had been away from church for five years, I knew God was the only hope for my daughter. The Holy Spirit began moving upon me to call upon my Lord and return to Him...I called my mother in my home state of Maine. She and others in my family notified churches in their area. My sister in California called the churches near her. All across America peo-

ple were praying for my daughter. I desperately needed a miracle...I was certain there was power in prayer.

Wednesday night came, I called Bethel Apostolic Church and was told, yes, they were having service that night. I told them about the accident and asked if they would pray...I arrived at Bethel in time for the evening service, went in, and sat on the back pew. As the music began, so did my tears. I could not hold all the sorrow and sadness. I began to cry and pour out my heart to Jesus, telling Him how sorry I was for leaving Him and praying that He would heal my child. The church family gathered around and prayed with me. The power of God was strong! The Lord cleansed and filled my soul, giving me a new outlook on life.

After service, I went home and put Lisa, our older daughter, to bed. I was expecting a call from my wife, and about 9:20 the phone rang. I was amazed as she began to tell me the news. Samantha had regained consciousness, she was moving her arms and legs, and she had even said three words! There was no doubt that the Lord Jesus had touched her.

Two weeks later, Samantha came home. One month later, she was walking and talking. Although the doctors predicted she would be blind, Samantha's sight returned to normal. Seven months after the accident, Samantha's doctors are amazed at her progress. No scars can be found from either the fractures to her skull or the hemorrhaging behind her eyes. [14]

There is healing for the body. There have been healing miracles all around the world for as long as God and man have existed. Remember, the word *incurable* is not in God's vocabulary. Jesus said that if a person could believe, all things were possible. This kind of belief or faith is described in Mark 11:22-23:

> And Jesus answering saith unto them, Have faith in God. For verily I say unto you, That *whosoever* shall say unto this mountain, Be thou removed, and be thou cast into the sea; and shall not doubt in his heart, but shall *believe* that those things which he saith shall come to pass; he shall have whatsoever he saith. Therefore I say unto you, What things soever ye desire, when ye pray, *believe* that ye receive them, and ye shall have them.

It is the will of God for people to prosper and be in health. III John 2 says, "Beloved, I wish above all things that thou mayest prosper and be in health, even as thy soul prospereth."

We are part of a world where there is suffering and sickness, as Kenneth Swanson wrote: "We all live in a fallen world, where illness, suffering, and pain are part of the fabric of existence." [15]

People need help. God has promised to help everyone that turns to Him. Why *not* ask Him for help in the time of sickness, disease, and pain?

"Prayer is the medicine expelling spiritual sickness, the foundation of the spiritual building, that which the soul is to the body."

S. Chrysotom

CHAPTER 7

THE HEALING POWER OF PRAYER FOR THE SOUL

The soul is "life" embodied in living human beings. The soul is the immortal spirit of man and will live forever. It is the moral and emotional nature, the seat of real life.

In the parable of the rich fool who said, "I will pull down my barns and build greater ones, and say to my soul, Soul, thou hast much goods laid up for many years; take thine ease, eat, drink, and be merry," Jesus showed that the soul was the eternal inner ear or consciousness to which individuals speak. The rich man spoke to his soul or inner spirit that would never die.

"But God said unto him, Thou fool, this night thy soul shall be required of thee: then whose shall those things be, which thou hast provided? So is he that layeth up treasure for himself, and is not rich toward God" (Luke 12:20-21).

Because he was rich only in tangibles and materialistic things and was a pauper in the area of the intangibles, he had no real power. God emphasized that the important thing was to have a rich relationship with Him, one that fed the soul, not just the shell or body of a man.

Another example of someone talking to herself was the little woman with an issue of blood. Matthew 9:21 says she spoke "within herself." She spoke to her soul or inner spirit that Jesus would heal her and because she believed it within herself, she was healed. Jesus said, "Thy faith hath made thee whole."

Genesis 2:7 says that God breathed into man and he became a living soul. He came alive! Soul and life are synergestically interwoven together. Where once was dead clay, immovable lips and empty eyes, there came a warmth into the body, blood started flowing, lips started moving and eyes started expressing emotions.

The soul is the inner yearnings of a person. Inside the heart of every human being there is a search for the Owner of the spirit that has been breathed into them. They are made immortal by God's breath and are fulfilled when they choose to let God come and dwell within them, not just as the breath of natural life, but with the breath of His spiritual life.

That is why Jesus came, so that humanity could have the spiritual breath of God breathed into them and He could dwell inside of them.

To reiterate a portion of Chapter 4, when Jesus ascended into the heavens, He told the people to go and tarry for the Spirit which would be sent to them. Luke describes what they were doing while they were waiting. "These all continued with one accord in prayer and supplication" (Acts 1:14). Suddenly after ten days, a sound as of a rushing mighty wind filled the house where they were sitting, and they were all filled with the gift of the Holy Spirit which was evidenced by the speaking with other tongues.

The soul is enlarged by prayer. The soul must have contact with God's Spirit or the soul will be miserable, depressed and fearful. Prayer is the method God has chosen for the soul to commune with its Creator. If there is no communication, there is emptiness. King David of ancient days described the longings of his soul: "O God, thou art my God; early will I seek thee: my soul thirsteth for thee, my flesh longeth for thee in a dry and thirsty land, where no water is" (Psalm 63:1).

Jesus said,

If any man thirst, let him come unto me, and drink. He that believeth on me, as the scripture hath said, out of his belly shall flow rivers of living water. (But this spake he of the Spirit, which they that believe on him should receive) (John 7:37-39).

The soul cannot be satisfied with anything less than pure living water, which is the Spirit of God.

This is illustrated by the story of the battle of El Alamein which had raged fiercely through the hours of the day when the heat was most intense on the sands of North Africa. When it seemed that the British could hold out no longer, they were suddenly surprised to see the German army throw up their hands in surrender. They came stumbling in, with parched protruding tongues and thick swollen lips, begging for water.

What had happened was that, as they overran the previous British position, the German soldiers discovered a newly constructed water main there, and they shot holes in it and drank deeply. The trouble was that the main was not in use for fresh water. It was being tested out by pumping seawater through it. What the Germans drank unknowingly was water from the Mediterranean Sea. The more they drank, the greater was their thirst in the battle.

It is the same way with the soul. The inner man can only be completely satisfied by being filled with God's Spirit, communing with Him, and being touched with things of eternal value.

Your soul is you. It is your pulsating emotions and feelings; it is the very fiber of your being. Inside of you is a war going on for your soul. The dark, sinister evil force of Satan would like to lower your spirits, corrode your mind, and put out your fire of enthusiasm. Christ came to do the opposite. He came to give you life, freedom and purpose. The paradox is that Satan wants you to drink his water, for his water will kill you, but the more you drink of it, the thirstier you become for the real thing. The sad thing is, not everyone finds it.

Carl Jung, the founder of the school of analytical psychology, was also impressed by the fact that neuroses were caused by the battle between two warring cerebral agents: "What drives people to war with themselves is the intuition or the knowledge that they consist of two persons in opposition to one another. The conflict may be between the sensual and the spiritual man....It is what Fault means when he says, 'Two souls, alas, dwell in my breast.'"[1]

In writing to the Romans, Paul describes two warring forces within his own mind before he was freed by the Holy Spirit. He dramatically describes the greater power of the carnal force nineteen centuries before the birth of psychiatry:

"My own behaviour baffles me. For I find myself not doing what I really want to do but doing what I really loathe. Yet surely if I do things that I really don't want to do it cannot be said that 'I' am doing them at all—it must be sin that has made its home in my nature. (And indeed, I know from experience that the carnal side of my being can scarcely be called the home of good!) I often find that I have the will to do good, but not the power. That is, I don't accomplish the good I set out to do, and the evil I don't really want to do I find I am always doing. Yet if I do things that I don't really want to do then it is not, I repeat, 'I' who do them, but the sin which has made its home within me...This is in continual conflict with my conscious attitude, and makes me an unwilling prisoner to the law of sin and death. In my mind I am God's willing servant, but in my own nature I am bound fast, as I say, to the law of sin and death. It is an agonizing situation, and who on earth can set me free from the clutches of my own sinful nature?" [2]

True freedom is released to people through the realm of the Spirit. Jesus said, "Ye shall know the truth and the truth shall make you free" (John 8:32). Jesus also said He was truth. "I am the way, the truth, and the life; no man cometh unto the Father, but by me" (John 14:6). Freedom comes by being filled with God's Spirit and making right choices.

In the quest of life everyone will from time to time battle against negative forces that seek to debase and enslave them. What happens to the individual who faces these debilitating emotions will be determined by which voice he listens to or who wins the war on the inside.

Some of the emotions found in the Scriptures which affect the soul either negatively or positively are as follows:

Discouragement:
"...the *soul* of the people was much *discouraged* because of the way" (Numbers 21:4).

Grief:
"And David was greatly distressed; for the people spake of stoning him, because the *soul* of all the people was *grieved*" (I Samuel 30:6).

Longing:
"And the *soul* of king David *longed* to go forth unto Absalom" (II Samuel 13:39).

Loyalty:
"And it came to pass, when he had made an end of speaking unto Saul, that the *soul* of Jonathan was *knit* with the *soul* of David, and Jonathan loved him as his own *soul*" (I Samuel 18:1).

Vexation:
"And when she came to the man of God to the hill, she caught him by the feet: but Gehazi came near to thrust her away. And the man of God said, Let her alone; for her *soul* is *vexed* within her" (II Kings 4:27).

Bitterness:
"Wherefore is light given to him that is in misery, and life unto the *bitter* in *soul*" (Job 3:20).

Anguish:
"Men groan from out of the city, and the *soul* of the *wounded* crieth out" (Job 24:12).

Fear:
"And *fear* came upon every *soul*" (Acts 2:43).

Weariness:
"My *soul* is *weary* of my life" (Job 10:1).

Joy:
"My *soul* shall be *joyful* in the Lord" (Psalm 35:9).

Love:
"And thou shalt *love* the Lord thy God with all thy heart, and with all thy *soul*, and with all thy mind, and with all thy strength: this is the first commandment" (Mark 12:30).

Cast down:
"Why art thou *cast down*, O my *soul*?" (Psalm 42:5).

Because emotions affect the soul each individual person must decide whether the emotion makes him bitter or better. How can a person receive help with managing intense feelings? The following six things will set the soul free from that which chains it. They will expand the soul, increase the will power to do that which is good, and help the individual make choices that will lift the soul to a higher level:

1. *The Word of God*
"The *law* of the Lord is perfect, converting the *soul*: the *testimony* of the Lord is sure, making wise the simple" (Psalm 19:7).

"Wherefore lay apart all filthiness and superfluity of naughtiness, and receive with meekness the engrafted *word*, which is able to *save your souls*" (James 1:21).

2. *The Lord*
"Behold, the eye of the *Lord* is upon them that fear him, upon them that hope in his mercy; To deliver their *soul* from death, and to keep them alive in famine. Our *soul* waiteth for the *Lord:* he is our help and our shield" (Psalm 33:18-19).

"The *Lord* redeemeth the *soul* of his servants; and none of them that trust in him shall be desolate" (Psalm 34:22).

"Rejoice the *soul* of thy servant: for unto thee, *O Lord*, do I lift up my *soul*" (Psalm 86:4).

"The *Lord* is my shepherd: I shall not want. He restoreth my *soul*..." (Psalm 23:1,3).

3. *Following His ways*
"Thus saith the Lord, Stand ye in the ways, and see, and ask for the old paths, where is the good *way*, and walk therein, and ye shall find *rest* for your *souls*" (Jeremiah 6:16).

4. *Prayer*
"The Lord is good unto them that *wait* for him, to the *soul* that *seeketh* him" (Lamentations 3:25).

5. *God's Spirit*
"Seeing ye have purified your *souls* in obeying the truth through the *Spirit*... " (I Peter 1:22).

"Hereby know we that we dwell in him, and he in us, because he hath given us of his *Spirit*" (I John 4:13).

When people are filled with God's Spirit, they are filled with light. Jesus said, "I am the light of the world: he that followeth me shall not walk in darkness, but shall have the light of life" (John 8:12).

> If there is light in the soul,
> There will be beauty in the person.
> If there is beauty in the person,
> There will be harmony in the house.
> If there is harmony in the house,
> There will be order in the nation.
> If there is order in the nation,
> There will be peace in the world.

Chinese Proverb

A soul filled with God's Spirit is a soul on fire with love and life. "For in him we live, and move, and have our being...For we are also his offspring" (Acts 17:28).

"...God is love: and he that dwelleth in love dwelleth in God, and God in him (I John 4:16).

6. *Pleasant words*

Proverbs 16:24 says, "*Pleasant words* are as an honeycomb, sweet to the *soul*, and health to the bones."

Words can bring warmth, inspiration and a feeling of power into your soul. What better way to bring words into your soul than by stories that make you want to live again.

Stories are words linked together to create wonder or to make one ponder deep subjects of the heart. It is good to fill the mind with stories that lift the heart and that fire the brain with challenge and hope. David of old said, "Let the words of my mouth, and the meditations of my heart, be acceptable in thy sight, O Lord, my strength, and my redeemer" (Psalm 19:14).

Read stories in the Holy Bible that increase your faith; read other literature and good stories that make you want to be a better person. Mull over the words and let them bring sweetness to your soul.

It is important how you treat your soul or your inner man. The soul will either live forever in heaven or suffer eternal torment, according to the decisions of the person in whom the soul dwells. Ezekiel 18:4 says, "The soul that sinneth, it shall die." Death here is not extinction, for the soul is separated from the body at the time of physical death to await the final judgment of all the inhabitants of the earth. The destination of the soul will be decided by God Himself at that time.

Dr. Wernher von Braun, well-known for his part in the U.S. space program, says he has "essentially scientific" reasons for believing in life after death. He explained,

> Science has found that nothing can disappear without a trace. Nature does not know extinction. All it knows is transformation. If God applies the fundamental principle to the most minute and insignificant parts of the universe, doesn't it make sense to assume that He ap-

plies it to the masterpiece of His creation—the human soul? I think it does. [3]

The blackest soul can be made clean through an encounter with Jesus Christ. There are millions that can attest to this fact; two especially are Saul of Tarsus and Starr Dailey.

Saul was a learned man who studied at the feet of Gamaliel, the great teacher, but became possessed with murdering and killing people that believed the truth of Jesus. He was ruthless, hard and merciless, until the day he was traveling on the road to Damascus. Out of heaven came a light so bright that it knocked Saul to the earth, and he heard a voice which said, "Saul, Saul, why persecutest thou me?"

"He said, Who art thou, Lord? And the Lord said, I am Jesus whom thou persecutest...." (Acts 9:5). Saul, in shock, arose from the earth and went into the city and was blind for three days and nights. While he was there, Ananias came to him because the Lord had visited him in a vision and told him to go into the street called Straight and inquire "for one called Saul, of Tarsus: for, behold, he prayeth" (Acts 9:11). One minute Saul was murdering, the next minute he was praying—all because of an encounter with Jesus Christ.

After being filled with the Lord's Spirit and being baptized in his name, Saul's name was changed to Paul, and he became such a dynamo that he shook his world. Letters he wrote to the churches were inspired by God to be a part of the New Testament to bless each generation of people, to instruct, inspire and teach how to live God's way. Author Catherine Marshall shares the story of Starr Daily in the book, *God Ventures*. At age 16 Starr's only ambition was to build a reputation as a dangerous man. He dreamed of the time when the police would refer to him with a shudder. Then in 1924, in a courtroom in the Midwest, the judge sentenced him to a major prison for the third time.

In prison Starr evolved a plan to instigate a prison riot. The deputy warden was to be seized and used as a shield and hostage. Someone betrayed him and told the authorities about the plan, and Starr was sentenced to the dungeon. Most strong men could not survive "the hole" for more than fifteen days.

It was winter, and the walls of the dank cell seeped moisture. At 6:00 every morning, Starr would be left hanging in handcuffs for twelve hours.

By the last day in the cuffs, Starr could no longer stand on his feet which were blackened with congealed blood. For weeks after that, he was allowed to lie on the icy stone floor—emaciated, unspeakably filthy, near death. Mired in the lowest hell imaginable, only hate was keeping him alive.

Then there came a moment when the man on the floor was too weak to hate. Through that momentary opening crept a strange new thought: *"All of my life I have been a dynamo of energy. What might have happened if I had used that energy for something good?"*

Then the thought faded. *"It's too late now; I'm dying."* There followed a half-waking, half-sleeping state of unconsciousness. This was followed by disconnected dreams, like mists floating across the brain. Finally, the dreams began to take on meaning. Suddenly Starr seemed to be in a garden. At one end of the garden a great white-gray rock jutted out. Then Jesus Christ, the Man whom he had been trying to avoid all his life, was coming towards him. Now He stood face to face with Starr, looking deep into his eyes, as if penetrating to the bottom of his soul. Love of a quality that he had never before felt was drawing the hate out of his heart; it was like extracting poison from an infected wound.

There followed another dream in which all the people Starr had ever injured passed before his eyes. One by one, he poured out his love to them. Then all who had injured him appeared, and on them too he bestowed the love needed to restore and to heal. The love flowed from beyond him and poured through him in a torrent of caring and ecstatic gratitude.

When he returned to consciousness, the cell did not look the same. Its grim grayness was gone. For him it was illuminated with a warm light. His feelings were different. The prison environment no longer had the power to give him pain, only joy.

Because of this encounter with Christ, Starr was released from prison five years ahead of the time set for his release. He went on to write over eight books and lectured all over the nation. His knowledge of the criminal mind contributed valuably to the rethinking of prison techniques. A blackened soul that knew only hate became a soul filled with love and care, all because a man had an encounter with Jesus Christ while lying half-dead on the cold, frozen floor of a dungeon in a prison.

An unknown author expressed it well in the following words: "The man who bows the lowest in the presence of God stands the straightest in the presence of sin." [4]

" Trust in the Lord with all thine heart, and lean not unto thine own understanding. In all thy ways acknowledge him, and he shall direct thy paths."

Proverbs 3:5-6

CHAPTER 8

GUIDANCE THROUGH PRAYER FOR EVERYDAY LIFE

Life's problems become too great for the human mind, soul and body to carry alone. God has ordained a plan to help humanity. It is simply, "Ask, and it shall be given you" (Matthew 7:7). It does not matter to God how great the need. He wants you to ask for help in the time of crisis and in the happenings of everyday life.

Life is not over, when you have God on your side. He can help you begin again. He can give you inspiration, walk you through an emergency, be with you in an accident, show you how to make a business failure turn into a success, or just help you every day whether life is normal or in crisis. Nothing is too big for Him to handle, but He wants everyone to ask in prayer; that is His plan.

Everett Jansen told a story that would benefit all to hear. Everett was a restaurant owner in Los Angeles who built a hole-in-the-wall "beanery" into a large and profitable business because he took Jesus Christ into partnership—literally. Previously, with apparently ample capital, he'd tried to conduct a large restaurant without Jesus Christ's aid, and had failed.

In the successful partnership, Jesus was the adviser. Jansen followed His instructions, and did the daily jobs. Each morning before he went to market at 3 a.m. to do his buying, he shut his eyes briefly and asked: "Jesus, what would You have me do today?"

Here is his story as he told of how he turned failure into success.

My first big restaurant failed because I didn't understand how to pray. Instead of asking Jesus what to do, I'd plead with Him to help me do something I wanted to do. I used to pray that He'd help me save my pride, humble my enemies, outsmart my competitors. I used to spend long, weary hours after I'd gone to bed at night, working out some scheme or other, then I'd kneel and ask Jesus to help me put it over.

I slept poorly, ate poorly. I became nervous and irritable. I felt that none of my prayers was really answered. I became bitter and despondent. I fought with my suppliers. My help became so jittery that customers felt it, and stayed away. My efforts and prayers became more frantic. The day came at last, when customers were so few that I had to close the doors. I opened a little beanery down on Main Street. Business was slow, and I had time to think. I realized, gradually, that my prayers had become only routine supplications. They'd failed to break through the fear and misery surrounding me, and had kept my spirit from reaching through into the divine essence that fills all space.

One evening as I sat behind an empty counter watching people—many of whom must have been hungry—walk past my little place without a glance, I suddenly felt I could endure it no longer. I realized I'd lost faith in myself, and in God. I dropped my head on my arms and cried, "O God!"

My cry must have been a prayer. At any rate, I grew calm, and sat there analyzing my situation. I was broke. My dream of a successful business was gone. My pride was crushed. I felt I'd lost the respect of my wife, and confidence of my friends. If ever a man was whipped, I was that man. I couldn't see how a man with my years of experience as cook, waiter, and buyer for a restaurant chain; my detailed knowledge of the intricacies of the restaurant business; my reasonable amount of capital–could fail–even against the hard competition among Los Angeles restaurants. Somewhere, I'd gone wrong–but where?

It was days before I found the answer, but find it, I did. My stumbling-block was the same one that I believe thousands of Christian business men trip over every year: *I hadn't been able to reconcile Jesus' teaching of brotherly love with the bitter competition of the business world.*

Instead of loving my competitors, I'd been hating them, tricking them, trying to force them out of business. I'd spent hours, days and months fighting, when I should have been building.

I came to realize that the apparent successes of godless business men were only temporary, at best. I knew from my own experience that they were victims of worries, frustrations and fears. And I knew with certainty, that godless businesses must fall, finally, just as godless nations and godless leaders must fall.

With Jesus directing one's business, there's no fear, no uncertainty, no darkness. Jesus said: "I am the light of the world: he that followeth me shall not walk in the darkness, but shall have the light of life." When we operate in accordance with God's laws, a divine warmth and brightness permeates us; we are filled with peace. [1]

Lloyd B. Wilhide of Keymar, Maryland, shares a miracle that happened to him while in a crisis on just an ordinary day. His story is told in the May 1982 issue of *Guideposts:*

"Ask and it shall be given you," Jesus said. I've always believed this, but never so totally as the day of the accident in 1978.

I was 75 years old. The grass on our 121-acre dairy farm needed cutting, so I hitched a set of mower blades to my tractor and went to work. The tractor was huge, and for added traction on our up-and-down Maryland terrain, its ear wheels were filled with 500 pounds of fluid, and a 200-pound weight hung from each hub.

When I finished the job, I was on a slight uphill grade near our chicken house. I switched off the ignition and climbed down from the high seat. I was unfastening the mower blades when the tractor started moving backward.

I tried to twist around and jump up on the seat, but I didn't make it. The tractor's drawbar hit me in the knees, knocking me flat, and the 700-pound left wheel rolled over my chest and stopped on top of it. I struggled for breath. The pain was agonizing. I knew I was facing death, and I made my request.

"Please, God," I begged, "release me."

At that moment the tractor began to move. It went forward enough to free my chest, and—to my astonishment—it moved *uphill!*

My dog, and then a farmhand, found me; and after six broken ribs, two fractures and 12 days in the hospital I was back home, talking with the Maryland state trooper called to investigate the accident. "I won't try to explain it officially," he told me. "Why, a dozen men couldn't have moved that tractor off you."

Twelve men or 1200, it didn't matter. Asking God's help did.

Asking God's help, helped win the Revolutionary War. One day a farmer approaching the camp at Valley Forge heard an earnest voice. On coming nearer, he saw George Washington on his knees, his cheeks wet with tears, praying to God.

The farmer returned home and said to his wife, "George Washington will succeed! George Washington will succeed! The Americans will secure their independence."

"What makes you think so, Isaac?" asked his wife.

The farmer replied, "I heard him pray, Hannah, out in the woods today, and the Lord will surely hear his prayer. He will, Hannah; thee may rest assured He will." [2]

When human beings can realize that, although they are finite, God is not, then they will be able to receive His help. God is supernatural and has the power to do all things. This is manifested in the story told by John L. Sherrill about an incident that happened in 1922, in the life of H. B. Garlock. They went to Africa as missionaries to the Pahns, a small tribe in the interior of Liberia.

While there one of their workers was captured by cannibal enemies. When Garlock received the urgent word that he would need to free his helper or else his helper would be eaten, he began praying that God would help him and show him what to do.

As he walked to the village of cannibals, he saw a wooden fence which ran around the cluster of huts. Garlock peeked cautiously through and saw that one of the huts had sentries posted before it. Two men carrying spears squatted outside in the dust. Their hair was braided in long pigtails, their front teeth were filed to a point.

That would be the prison, Garlock decided. Walking as straight and as tall as he could, he strode directly toward the prison hut. The guards were too astonished to stop him. He walked between them and ducked inside the hut. Outside the guards begin to shout. He heard feet slap against the packed earth as others ran to join them. In the dark interior Garlock crawled forward until his hands touched a figure tied to the center pole of the hut. He cut the man loose and dragged him through the door, but that was as far as he got. There in the courtyard was a yelling, threatening crowd armed with knives, spears and hatchets.

From out of one of the huts stepped the chief who was joined by the witch doctor, and walking towards Garlock the witch doctor began to harangue him; this went on for about an hour. Then there was silence while the people waited for something to happen.

> Garlock did not know one word of the Pahn language. The crowd began to grow restless. Garlock prayed, "Lord, show me what to do. Send your Spirit to help me."
>
> Suddenly Garlock began to shake violently. This frightened him as he did not want the others to see that he was afraid. But with the trembling came a sense of the Holy Spirit. Words of Jesus came to him: "Take no thought what ye shall speak, neither do ye premeditate; but whatsoever shall be given to you in that hour, that

speak ye; for it is not ye that speak but the Holy Ghost."

Garlock felt a strange boldness. He took a deep breath and began to speak. From his lips came a flow of words which he did not understand. Garlock saw the natives lean forward, enthralled. He saw that the words had a stirring effect on those who listened. He knew beyond a doubt that he was speaking to the Pahns in their own language.

For twenty minutes Garlock talked to the Pahns. Then, as suddenly as the speech-power came, it vanished, and Garlock knew that he had come to the end of his discourse. [3]

What happened next was a miracle. After going through the ritual of killing a rooster and sprinkling blood on the foreheads of Garlock and the prisoner, the cannibals released them to return home. The chief even supplied two of his own men to guide them the first part of the journey.

Life is not always easy; it is sometimes very harsh and difficult. The great preacher Peter Marshall prayed the following prayer when he was under pressure, which would help everyone if they would pray the same way when trouble came:

> Our Father, when we long for life without trials and work without difficulties, remind us that oaks grow strong in contrary winds and diamonds are made under pressure.

With stout hearts may we see in every calamity an opportunity and not give way to the pessimism that sees in every opportunity a calamity. [4]

Writer Patience Strong beautifully penned the following words, and challenged people to kneel and pray and ask for guidance to help along the way:

At the gateway of the year now let us kneel to pray—asking God to bless us ere we go upon our way....We dare not take one step along the road that lies ahead—without a prayer for guidance on the path that we must tread.

Let us pray for strength, endurance, courage, fortitude—so that we may venture out with hope and faith renewed...mighty weapons, final victory. [5]

"All who call on God in true faith, earnestly from the heart, will certainly be heard, and will receive what they have asked and desired."

Martin Luther

CHAPTER 9

MODERN-DAY ANSWERS TO PRAYER

There are millions of prayers that have been answered in many continents, countries and counties. God is faithful and He does all things well. He makes no mistakes and has all power in His hands. He came to bring deliverance, healing and salvation, and to set people free from the domination of evil. Satan on the other hand has a plan to kill, destroy and steal from humanity. Because he was kicked out of heaven and destined for the bottomless pit to live forever and ever at the end of the world, he desires to take as many with him as he possibly can. He seeks to enslave, bind, intoxicate, chain and bring pain, hate and evil to all. Jesus came to bring freedom and abundant life.

Jesus instituted a plan for receiving good things from God. He said in Matthew 7:7, "Ask, and it shall be given you; seek, and ye shall find; knock, and it shall be opened unto you." He asked them to reason things out: if a son asked bread of his father, would he give him a stone? If he asked for fish, would he give him a serpent? He then said, "If ye...know how to give good gifts unto your children, how much more shall your Father which is in heaven give good things to them that ask him?" (Matthew 7:11).

Since 1991, God has opened a door for a group of women to have public prayer on KCJH, our local Christian radio station, and I am privileged to be the leader of that session. Every Wednesday morning from 10:00 to 11:00, we gather in the KCJH studio and begin with "praise" reports and a special Word from the Holy Bible. The phone lines are jammed the whole time and God is answering many of our prayers. Many people take time to pray with us, whether they are in their cars, homes or workplaces—some even listen in the jails and prisons. Most of all, there is a tangible presence of the Lord God that fills the atmosphere and we tingle with His closeness.

The Scripture passage found in Mark 11:22-24 (see Chapter 6) has been read many times to impart faith to believe God for answers.

There have been hundreds of prayers answered and I have shared a few of them in other publications. Since God is able to do exceedingly, abundantly above all we ask or think, the answers to prayer included in this chapter should not shock us; instead our souls should magnify, glorify and exalt the Lord, for He is the healer of all dis-

THE HEALING POWER OF PRAYER

ease, He sets the captive free, He is the all in all. Whatever the need is, He is the answer, but we must ask and only believe.

On May 22, 1996, we received a picture of a seven-year-old boy along with a letter from Kara King from Minnesota who was attending college in Stockton, California, where the prayer group meets. She wrote,

> My cousin, Timmy Eishen, was very sick at the beginning of this school year. My parents called and asked me to pray. Timmy's liver quit working for no apparent reason. He turned yellow and was in terrible pain. The doctors said his heart would give out the next day unless a new liver came. I had you pray and I got a call the next day saying he'd received a perfect liver and they put it in. He was fine. He went home and a few weeks later his liver rejected and he was rushed into the hospital. He fell into a coma and was sick with very much pain. I was told that if they couldn't make it work, he would die. We prayed again. The next news I heard was that the liver was working again in perfect order and they were giving him anti-rejection drugs. He had been healed again!
>
> A couple months ago I got news that the drugs had given him brain cancer. This cancer spread throughout his body and he was in a coma again. He was so far in, the doctors said he would have severe brain damage, not be able to talk, or see, and may have a serious learning disability—that's if he lived. They began chemotherapy and radiation. He got worse and worse

and I put his name in for prayer again. He now has got a perfect brain, no damage, no disabilities, no problems seeing or talking. He was completely healed! All cancer was gone. The Lord has saved his life many times. Three distinct times they have pronounced his impending death. The three times, the Lord has healed.

Two weeks ago, Timmy got a very large lump on his forehead that was black and blue and his mom, Carole, rushed him to the emergency room. They didn't know what to tell her, but more appeared on his face. I asked you to pray and the lumps disappeared. The doctors are confounded! They admit they've never seen anything like this before. They say they can't predict anything anymore.

This has been a witness to Timmy's parents of God's power. I am eternally grateful for the ladies' prayers. They had already planned his funeral. I'm thanking God he didn't have to use it.

On May 29, 1996, Anna Stevens called in with a praise report. She had called in to ask prayer to help her find a job, and while we were praying, she was healed of growths on her hand and foot. She said she watched them go down before her eyes.

We received a praise report from Eleanor in New Mexico. She had pneumonia and a collapsed lung, and even died on the operating table. Prayer was made and God raised her up and she is fine.

Tara called in with a praise report. She had a syndrome that had no cure. The doctors thought she needed a bone marrow transplant, but after prayer was made, she was made completely well: no syndrome, no bone marrow transplant, no cancer.

Jocelyn Vega called in with a praise report. She said a year ago she had called in so she would be able to have a child; she had been unable to. A year later she had a son and when he was almost a year old, he started having medical problems. The doctors suspected an overactive thyroid. Since prayer was made all his tests came back negative and he is fine.

Leonard from Galt called in to praise the Lord. He had broken his kneecap and had no insurance. His medical bill was $35,000. The praise was that the Lord had healed the kneecap beautifully and the bill had all been taken care of. *Remember: the doctors dress the wound, but God heals it.*

Yolanda called in for prayer because her baby was breech. Two days later she called in to say she had gone to the doctor and the baby had turned.

Ken called in with a praise report on July 13, 1994. He had called in for a financial blessing and on the same day he went to his mailbox and there was a check that he was not expecting. He does not know why he received it.

Lula called in November 23, 1994, to say she went to work feeling ill, but as soon as she tuned in to the prayer hour, she felt the anointing come over her and felt completely healed. This happens frequently.

Nine-year-old Reuben had a bad headache; when he heard prayer over the air, it completely disappeared

Pam called in for prayer—she needed money for groceries. The ladies prayed and moments after prayer her husband called; he had been given a job that paid cash up front. She also had requested prayer for a friend who had a stroke and was paralyzed on one side. She was praising God because he was now walking and talking.

Linda called in and reported that the prayer that had been prayed for them had been answered: the $150,000 judgment that had come against them had been dropped.

Angie called in for an uncle who was running for District Judge in Idaho. She said, "Praise God, he won."

Cecilia had a blood disorder. Her platelets were low, but after prayer they started going up. She got out of the hospital the next day.

Thursday, May 26, 1994, Melody called in with a praise. The day before she had called for prayer for her house to be sold. It had been six months and hardly anyone had even looked at it. On Wednesday night at 9:00, someone knocked on the door and went through it and offered them just what they needed.

Paula Gooch went in for surgery to remove a cyst on her ovary which the doctors had seen on four sonograms. Prayer was made, and when the doctors made the incision, there was no cyst.

Harry Baker called in with a praise report. He had had a stroke and two weeks later after prayer, he was up and walking.

Debbie called in for her nephew, Brian, who was five years old. He had had surgery and developed an infection and high fever. Her praise was that while we were praying, the fever broke and he was able to take his medication and go home from the hospital shortly thereafter.

THE HEALING POWER OF PRAYER

Financial praise reports come in consistently. Esther called in for prayer. Their house was in foreclosure. After prayer, the Lord blessed them with the money they needed to bring everything up-to-date and they did not have to move. Ted called in to say that after prayer was made, his house got refinanced even though they did not qualify.

God can qualify anyone, He can heal, He can make cancers disappear; these are all small things for Him to do. There is no limit to His power.

Judy, who was on drugs for twenty years, is praising God for complete deliverance as a result of prayer.

Suzanne was diagnosed with breast cancer. When she went in for surgery, it was not cancer. She is praising God for her miracle. This happened to Laverna also; they opened her up, but could not find any cancer.

Tammy's daughter, Tosha, ran away from home. Tammy heard Psalm 102 read during prayer and took faith. Tosha called and said she would be home Friday.

Kathy called in to report that even though her doctors had not expected her to live, her heart had been healed. Two days after surgery she was eating solid food.

We prayed for the marriage of Manuel and Terri who have been separated for about eight months. Monday night he asked her to dinner and told her he was not happy with his "other situation." They had dinner together again Tuesday night. This was a miracle.

Pastor J.P. Feld from Florida called in three praise reports. One person was healed of a growth on the bladder; one week it showed up on an x-ray; the next week after prayer, it was completely gone. We anointed and prayed over two handkerchiefs and sent them to Pastor Feld for two other people. A man was bleeding internally so heavily it was clotting. The day he received the anointed handkerchief the bleeding stopped. The culture that the doctor sent to the lab was cancerous and while it was in the lab the culture was healed. Doctors said it was a miracle; they had never seen anything like it before.

A brother-in-law got a handkerchief from Pastor Feld and gave it to a woman who was going into surgery that morning for breast cancer. The doctors took one more x-ray on the way into surgery and the cancer had shrunk, so they sent her home and told her to come back a week later. She did and when they took another x-ray, the cancer was completely gone.

We received a card with a tiny baby's picture and inside was this message:

Dear Wednesday Morning Prayer Group,
Ten months ago I phoned and asked for prayer for my daughter, who has wanted to have a baby for many years. She got pregnant the month after I phoned. Thank you so much for all of the people who come together and pray for our needs. God bless you! I'm sending a picture of my new granddaughter.
Love, Barbara.

We received a letter dated August 6, 1994, from Sandy Guerrero who lives in Napa, California.

THE HEALING POWER OF PRAYER

[On] May 3, 1993 I was told by my doctor that I had almost lost all my amniotic fluid; I was 21 weeks along in my pregnancy. The doctor gave me a 10% chance at first to successfully have the baby, then the odds went even lower as my situation got worse. I was also at great risk of getting an infection which if not caught in time would put my life in danger. My sister had requested prayer for me on the prayer hour on May 12. May 17th she called and said she was requesting again. She called back later and let me hear your voice praying for me over the radio. She had taped it; I felt the Holy Ghost! July 9, 1993, my baby girl weighed in at 4 pounds and she was 16 inches long and she was not deformed and her lungs were developed. Praise God all is well!

We received a letter dated July 6, 1996, from a lady.

Just to let you know how much you are appreciated. A couple of years ago I called the radio station on Wednesday at prayer time with a very important request. No hesitation, you helped and joined in prayer for a friend dying with brain tumors. Two days later he was scheduled for surgery. They prepared him and the doctor said, "We need to take one more x-ray before we begin." Praise the Lord! The doctor found **no** tumors!!! Hallelujah!!! And even today he is still healed."

Prayer was made in March 1996 for Margarita and Frank in Japan. A praise report came in on April 8, 1996, concerning Frank, who had lyme disease. After prayer he received his test results, and they were negative.

Stephanie called in with a praise report. She was in a coma for two-and-one-half months. Her friends called in for prayer. She is now out of her coma and at home recovering.

Kelley called in January 1996, for her mother who was diagnosed with breast cancer. She was undergoing more tests, and her doctor thought it had spread to the bones. After much prayer, all tests came back negative–no cancer.

A mother brought her nine-year-old daughter who was in much pain to the radio station. The doctors were going to have to do surgery because her intestines were plugged up. After prayer the pain went away and she did not have surgery.

Pam had a pain in her chest for two months that would not leave. The ladies prayed on June 12, 1996, and on June 26, she called in with a praise report that it left and had not come back.

Kyle, who had a mysterious illness and was sick for five days, could not eat and had a fever; his mother called in and two hours later Kyle was healed and eating.

Dennis, who had been an alcoholic for 26 years, called in on February 7, 1996, and said he was completely delivered from the thirst for alcohol after prayer was made for him.

THE HEALING POWER OF PRAYER

The mother of a 17-year-old boy who had only six months to live called in and said after prayer was made he had been healed of cancer. When the doctor opened him up, the cancer was gone. His words were, "It was like someone walked in and removed the devil."

These are a few of the miracles the Lord is performing all in answer to fervent prayers by people who care. God is on the throne and has promised to do great things for people if they will only believe. The key is believing, for Jesus said over and over while He was on earth, "Thy faith hath made thee whole." There is no question as to whether He is able to answer prayer, the question is whether we are able to believe Him to do so.

Some people have trouble believing that God can heal in this modern day. But unbelief has been in existence since the beginning of time. Saint Augustine who doubted the validity of healing prayer stated in his early writings that Christians should not look for the continuance of the healing gift. But in 424 A.D., a brother and sister came to his town of Hippo, seeking healing of convulsive seizures. They came every day to Augustine's church to pray for healing. Nothing happened until the second Sunday before Easter. The young man was in the crowded church, praying. Augustine was still in the vestibule, when the young man fell down as if dead. People nearby were seized with fear, but the next moment he got up and stood staring back at them, perfectly normal and fully cured.

Slowly Augustine's doubt began to crumble after he talked with the young man at length. On the third day after Easter, he had the brother and sister stand on the choir

MODERN-DAY ANSWERS TO PRAYER

steps, where the whole congregation could see them. He read a statement from the young man and then began a sermon on healing. Augustine was interrupted by shouts from the congregation, for the young woman had also fallen to the ground and was instantaneously healed. Once more she stood before the people, and, in Augustine's own words, "Praise to God was shouted so loud that my ears could scarcely stand the din." [1]

God still hears and answers the cries of a desperate heart. Sometimes there is a long wait until He answers, but He does answer as long as praise and faith is maintained in the waiting period.

THE HEALING POWER OF PRAYER

NOTES

Chapter 1
[1] Alexis Carrel, M.D., *Reader's Digest*, (Pleasantville, NY: Reader's Digest Assn., 1941), p. 36.
[2] Dr. William Wilson, *The Unlimited Power of Prayer*, Guideposts Associates, (Garden City, NY: Doubleday,1982) 128.
[3] Ibid., 130.
[4] Ibid., 132.
[5] Harvey Cox, *Fire from Heaven*, (Addison-Wesley Publishing Co.: Reading, MA, 1995), xvi.
[6] Ibid.

Chapter 2
[1] Paul Lee Tan, ThD., *Encyclopedia of 7,700 Illustrations: Signs of the Times* (Rockville, MD: Assurance Publishers, 1979), 1046.
[2] Larry Dossey, M.D., *Healing Words: The Power of Prayer and the Practice of Medicine*, (San Francisco, CA: HarperCollins Publishers, 1993).
[3] Ibid.
[4] Alexander Lake, *Your Prayers are Always Answered*, (New York, NY: Simon and Schuster, 1956), 208.
[5] Ibid., 222.
[6] Ibid., 223.
[7] Ibid., 225.
[8] Ibid., 227.
[9] Ibid., 214.
[10] Carrel, 34-35.
[11] Dale Carnegie, *How to Stop Worrying and Start Living*, (New York, NY: Simon & Schuster, 1948), 24.
[12] Herbert Benson, M.D. with William Proctor, *Your Maximum Mind*, (New York, NY: Times Books, 1987), 192.

Chapter 3
[1] Lillian Eichler Watson, ed. & comm., *Light from Many Lamps*, (New York, NY: Simon & Schuster, 1951), 66.
[2] Tan, 192.
[3] Ibid.
[4] Ibid., 1036.

[5] Ibid., 192.
[6] Ibid.
[7] Ibid.
[8] Ibid.
[9] Ibid.
[10] Ibid., 1042.
[11] Ibid., 192.
[12] Ibid.
[13] Ibid., 1619.
[14] Ibid.
[15] Ibid., 1618.
[16] Joseph S. Johnson, comp., *A Field of Diamonds* (Nashville, TN: Broadman Press, 1974), 122.
[17] Tan, 1620.
[18] Marie King, *The Gold Star Family Album*, Arthur and Nancy DeMoss, eds. (Old Tappan, NJ: Fleming H. Revell Co., 1968), 74.
[19] Tan, 1620.
[20] Ibid., 1045.
[21] Clinton T. Howell, ed., *Lines to Live By* (Nashville, TN: Thomas Nelson Publishers, 1972), p.167.
[22] Tan, 158.
[23] Johnson, 153.
[24] Tan, 1064.
[25] Helen Keller, *The Story of My Life*, (Garden City, NY: Doubleday & Co., Inc., 1954), 96-97
[26] Reader's Digest, 35.
[27] Watson, 43.
[28] Ibid.

Chapter 4
[1] Johnson, 153.
[2] Irene Buk Harrel, compiled by, *God Ventures*, (Plainfield, NJ: Logos International, 1970), 47.
[3] Leonard Ravenhill, *Revival God's Way*, (Minneapolis, Minnesota: Bethany House Publishers, 1983), 99.
[4] Ibid., 96.
[5] Andrew D. Urshan, *The Supreme Need of the Hour*, (Portland, OR: Apostolic Book Publishers, 1981), 123
[6] Ibid., 96.

[7] S.I. McMillen, M.D., *None of These Diseases*, (Westwood, NJ: Fleming H. Revell, 1963), 99.
[8] Watson, 62-63.
[9] Ibid., 64-65.
[10] Ibid., 65.
[11] Ibid., 65-66.
[12] Johnson, 155.
[13] Ibid.
[14] Carrell, 35.

Chapter 5
[1] Carnegie, 153.
[2] Ibid.
[3] Ibid.
[4] Ibid., 19.
[5] McMillen, 144.
[6] Carnegie, 20.
[7] Benson, 6-7.
[8] Ibid., 7-9.
[9] Ibid., 24-25.
[10] Ibid., 45-46.
[11] Ibid., 64.
[12] Ibid., 103.
[13] Howell, 175.
[14] Richard J. Foster, *Prayer*, (San Francisco, CA: Harper Collins Publishers, 1992), 219.

Chapter 6
[1] Carnegie, 253-254.
[2] McMillen, 67.
[3] Robert Ornstein, Ph.D. and David Sobel, M.D., *Healthy Pleasures*, (Reading, MA: Addison Wesley Publishing Co., Inc., 1989), 183, 186-187.
[4] Caryle Hirshberg & Marc Ian Barasch, *Remarkable Recovery*, (New York, NY: Riverhead Books, 1995), 22
[5] Ibid., 29.
[6] Ibid., 31.
[7] Ibid.
[8] Ibid., 119.
[9] Ibid.

[10] Ibid., 120.
[11] Ibid., 121.
[12] Ibid., 122.
[13] Tan, 944.
[14] Ester Hill, *Pentecostal Herald Magazine*, (St. Louis, MO: Pentecostal Publishing House, July 1992), 14.
[15] Foster, 207.

Chapter 7
[1] McMillen, 141.
[2] Ibid., 143.
[3] Tan, 378.
[4] Johnson, 155.

Chapter 8
[1] Lake, 158.
[2] Tan, 1037.
[3] Harrell, 16.
[4] Marshall, Guideposts Associates, *The Unlimited Power of Prayer*, 17.

Chapter 9
[1] Foster, 215.